AMERICAN FOOTBALL

AMERICAN FOOTBALL

THE FUTURE OF SOCCER IN THE UNITED STATES

AIDAN CHAPMAN

NDP

NEW DEGREE PRESS

AMERICAN FOOTBALL

The Future of Soccer in the United States

ISBN 978-1-64137-903-8 *Paperback*

978-1-64137-627-3 *Kindle Ebook*

978-1-64137-629-7 *Ebook*

CONTENTS

INTRODUCTION

I have been in love with soccer my entire life.

I still have vivid memories of playing the fittingly named "MicroSoccer," which is the equivalent version of rec soccer at my local parish. Three players from teams of five or six little kids, ranging from four to six years old, compete within the match to varying levels of intensity. It was common for teams to attain up to ten goals, sometimes even breaking the threshold of twenty if they played a particularly inadequate group of preschoolers.

There was also a vast diversity of skill levels. Some players would rack up in the double digits and lead their team to deserved glory. On the other end of the scale, some kids opted to pick dandelions near the corner flag rather than participate in a soccer match, which required running and sometimes even kicking a ball, or worse, having the ball kicked at *you*. It's easy to see why so many were turned off by such a heinous sport at such a young age.

I can still colorfully remember watching soccer with some of the people who influenced my life the most and directed my path to extreme soccer fanaticism. Elise was the first of a series of au pairs who worked for my family and shared their culture, and inevitably soccer, with me and the rest of my siblings and family. She hailed from Brazil or, as she would constantly remind us, "Brasil." As a Brazilian citizen, she was naturally a fan of the game. I only truly realized how universal the game was as I made a shopping trip with my dad to the mall where we picked up some bargain kits. The knockoffs were amazing. I could pretend to be a footballer from all around the world. I could pretend to be an Italian, English, Mexican, or when I felt especially daring, even an American footballer whenever I liked. Naturally, Elise especially prized the Brazilian kits and shared images of my nine-year-old brother and me clad in our very own yellow and green with all her friends back home.

Eventually, Elise left us for her newfound husband, but we continued to have a constant stream of au pairs, and thus soccer exposure, in my house as I grew up. Johanna the Austrian. Franzi, the German Dortmund fan. Adriana, a tremendous supporter of Real Madrid from Huesca, Spain.

My fondest memories of Franzi are directly connected to my memories of the 2014 men's World Cup in Brazil, the greatest of which happened when Germany, the eventual winners, faced home team Brazil in one of the most famous World Cup matches of all time.

As we sat down to watch the match from the floor of our living room, she said, "This should be a good match; I'm excited to see how Klose plays. I think he'll score today." Miroslav Klose, the German International striker, was on the verge of becoming the all-time top scorer for the country.

"Well Mesut Ozil is way better," my eleven-year-old self very eloquently replied. "I bet he'll score a hat trick," I continued confidently, even though Ozil is much more adept at creating goals as a passer rather than a striker.

"Either way, Germany will win," Franzi responded diplomatically, with her eyes fixed on the screen as the match kicked off. "I bet we'll win 3–1," she predicted. Her prediction soon proved to be pretty good as Germany began to dominate when Thomas Muller scored off a corner in the eleventh minute. And as Miroslav Klose wheeled away into a slide after his twenty-third-minute strike, she cheered with glee as Germany doubled their lead and the striker proved at least one of her predictions to be accurate. "Even if the game does finish with this scoreline," she added, "I will still have guessed the margin correctly. Two-nil would be great!" she continued, celebrating.

As the game continued and the eventual 7–1 trouncing of Brazil was finalized as the referee blew his whistle to signal the end of the ninety minutes plus stoppage, I had no idea that I had just had the pleasure of witnessing a game that would go down as one of the most historic World Cup games of all time. Not only had I been blessed to witness it firsthand, but I also witnessed it in the presence of a native fan of one of the two nations. Although I privately thought, *Had Elise been there instead, I don't think the mood would have been quite as celebratory.*

As the au pairs came and went, I became infatuated with the commonality of the sport. Everybody played it, not just the United States, and not just Britain. Around four billion people are involved with the sport in some capacity, whether through fandom or as a player. That is more than half of the world's population, which means enjoying soccer is potentially the most supported subjective stance presented anywhere. The endless possibilities provided by the worldliness of the game were enthralling.

**

Soccer, however, has not taken off within the United States the same way it took off within me. In the United States of America, Soccer is not the sport of the people. Soccer is not the sport of the masses. Soccer is the sport of the few and the privileged willing to pay to play the game.

In the streets of Sao Paulo, Amsterdam, or Accra, kids are learning the sport like a second language, hoping to become the next Pelé or Messi. On those same streets in the United States, kids are increasingly turning to other sports, such as basketball or football. Or even worse, they are removing themselves from athletic competition altogether and neglecting their playful sides.

Kids, especially those not born into money, are having a harder time getting into the sport. Whereas in Brazil or the Netherlands or Ghana, soccer has flourished in the streets, it has only been an option for Americans as a single critical feature. For Americans to fully engage in a soccer lifestyle, it has almost become a prerequisite that one's family must have a large checkbook to fund their kid's interest in the game.

The second problem in the United States that has led to the tremendous turnoff to American soccer is that Major League Soccer (MLS) has failed to enthrall Americans the same way the Premier League, or the Bundesliga, has drawn the attention of the English or the Germans. The shortcomings of MLS are in part due to the lower level of football in comparison to the aforementioned English Premier League or German Bundesliga.

For MLS and the United States National Team, and the sport, as a whole within the United States, to truly taste success, reform is necessary. To truly succeed, it's necessary to recognize shortcomings. The United States must acknowledge where they need to put in work and what work needs to be put forth.

**

Unlike so many adults who have made an effort to Americanize the sport in the last decade, I have grown up in the backward pay-to-play system, and I have experienced what it's like to face the prospect of sacrificing copious amounts of time and money just to play the sport you love. I also know what it's like to be a fan of the game. I have been following English soccer for the last four years. Lower league football fandom has opened my eyes to more truths of the sport than any boardroom meeting or Franchise expansion fee ever could.

The solution is not to Americanize soccer—quite the contrary, in fact. To facilitate the progression of the beautiful game within the United States, we must soccer-ize America.

The method is building the soccer ecosystems throughout the country and using that as the foundation for expanding the outreach of the sport, beyond a financial game to a community-based cohesive sport that unifies diverse groups. After all, America is the most diverse country in the world, so why aren't its sports as diverse?

This is a call to all those who hold a position of power within the American Soccer Community. We must conform to the European model, but with an American spin. There is no way to grow the sport further without taking into account the context of the sport's universality. We need to fix the American system and make the world's game America's game as well. We can do this by deviating from profit-based systems.

This is also a call to young soccer players. You have a choice to stick with the game. It is of the utmost importance that we foster those who are to be ushered into the next great generation of soccer players in the United States, rather than England, Brazil, or Germany. With your devotion and commitment to the game, the United States will become the next great footballing superpower.

If you believe in this mission to propel the United States further into the realm of European athletics, in the future of America as a footballing nation, and in the country's capacity to build a team that can dominate world football and excel at the World Cup—if you believe, read on.

PART 1

CHAPTER 1

EARLY HISTORY AND THE BEGINNING OF THE BEAUTIFUL GAME

How did we get here?

This philosophical question has been stumping humanity for eons, and in the case of soccer, it's not much easier to answer.

The game has its first known roots in China. While the sport has primarily flourished in Europe during the modern era and since the start of the nineteenth century, Chinese as early as the Han dynasty during the second and third centuries BCE were playing a game known as *Cuju,* which resembled the broad sport known as "football." The Chinese developed the roots of the game, which involved a ball and the use of all parts of the body except the hands. (Modern soccer permits use of all parts of the body except the hands and arms, which were permitted in the early Chinese game.)[1]

After initial roots in China, the spread of the beautiful game is hard to follow. In a world driven by extreme globalization, it's nearly impossible to imagine a world in which an idea as simple as soccer would take centuries to spread, but at the time, without the existence of mass transportation and stable long roads, it took a long time for ideas to disseminate.

It's possible that the game spread slowly from ancient China to the Mediterranean, but it's also possible that the game evolved independently in southern Europe. Either way, football found its way into the records and art of the Greek and Roman civilizations from the early first millennium CE.[2]

Once the game had taken root in Europe, football found its way into England, where the sport as we know it was born. In medieval times, mob football, or *shrove*, was the main manifestation of the game. During the early nineteenth century, the sport became more organized and was played primarily at colleges and universities by male students.[3]

Finally, in 1848 at Cambridge University, the students decided to set standards for the game that would be known as football. Before the standardization, the sport most resembled the modern sport of rugby football—in that the use of hands

---

1 "The history of football (soccer)," Footballhistory.org, accessed July 2, 2020.

2 Ibid.

3 Ibid.

was permitted and fouls were not regulated by an officiating body such as a referee.[4]

This led to a very physical sport that involved a lot of contact, and it had essentially no rules besides the objective of each team to reach the end line in some capacity by either scoring a goal or even reaching a landmark (similar to the modern touchdown of American football). The conference at Cambridge sought to establish guidelines on how to regulate the game. They defined fouls and limited the sport to the use of the entire body except for the hands and arms.[5]

This led to the development of a universal football governing body also known as the Football Association (FA), which would be the leading authority on all things football. The FA was founded in the Free Masons Tavern in London on October 26, 1863. Its main role was to implement the regulations and guidelines discussed by the students at Cambridge fifteen years earlier.[6]

***

To this day, The English FA regulates Association Football in England. This means they control the England national team. They are in charge of making sure that the Premier League, the English Football League (EFL), the Women's Premier League, and all other leagues are running smoothly. They are in charge of the finances of English football and work on

---

4 Ibid.

5 Ibid.

6 "The History of the FA," TheFA, accessed July 2, 2020.

investing that and forecasting the future of the game. They sponsor a domestic tournament every season called the FA Cup, which pins teams from every league in a bracket-style competition that runs parallel to the leagues.[7]

The United States has a similar organization called U.S. Soccer, which is in charge of similar tasks. They regulate and finance the development of the game through a series of committees, and they run the U.S. Open Cup as well as the country's various national teams.[8] The largest difference is in the quality of the management. U.S. Soccer has done a much worse job over the last five years preparing the nation's broad soccer ecosystem for the future of the game, the English FA, on the other hand, has done an excellent job growing the international success of English football.

***

At the 1863 meeting, the FA finalized the development of modern football, or association football as we know it today. They officially removed the use of hands and arms from the game and standardized rules involving new regulations on the use of hands and disallowing players from kicking or directly tackling opponents.[9]

---

7 "Driving Change with the FA Sustainability Team (Fast)," TheFA, accessed July 2, 2020; "The FA Strategic Plan 2016-2020," TheFA, accessed July 2, 2020; "FA Reports and Financial Statements," TheFA, accessed July 2, 2020.

8 "Governance," U.S. Soccer, accessed July 2, 2020.

9 Ben Johnson, "Association Football or Soccer," *Historic UK*, accessed July 2, 2020.

Obviously, the sudden shift in the game made some people who relied on those aspects of the game unhappy. The primary members of this faction were those who played a style of the game much more similar to modern rugby. After detaching themselves from the Football Association, they founded the Rugby Football Union in 1971.[10] The faction's fracture from the rest of football finalized the dissociation between modern association football and modern rugby football.

The development of association football in the United Kingdom is not dissimilar to that of American football in the United States. In the U.S., the game grew out of the same broad football that led to soccer and rugby. Not only did they come from the same place, but both sports were also first played in an organized manner at the university level. Cambridge's American counterparts, Princeton and Rutgers, played the first-ever college football game in 1869.[11]

In the 1880s, only a few years after the initial game, American colleges, much like the group of young men at Cambridge a couple of years prior, developed their own official rules. Walter Camp of Yale University was the main leader in campaigning for the final version of football to secede from the broad sport that evolved into rugby football, association football, and American football.[12]

Around this time, the term *soccer* also evolved from football and began the controversial argument between Americans

---

10 "The History of Rugby Union," BlackandBlue1871, accessed July 2, 2020.

11 Spencer Parlier, "College football history: Notable firsts and milestones," *NCAA.com*, January 31, 2020.

12 "Birth of Pro Football," Pro Football Hall of Fame, accessed July 2, 2020.

and the football countries of the world over what to call the beautiful game.

During the late mid-1800s, it was common slang for "-er" to be added onto the ends of words. This resulted in terms such as footer, sporter, rugger (rugby), and soccer. The term soccer was derived from the phrase "association football." The *soc* part comes from the *soc* within the word association while the *er* part of the word comes from the common slang of the time. The additional *c* was added to complete the word.[13]

When football became soccer in the 1800s, that moment marked the fork in divergent paths of evolution. While both sports began in the same place, they finally separated in the 1800s, making two distinct sports, with separate rule books determined by athletes from the respective sports at university. From this moment on, the sports moved further and further apart, and there is no greater proof than in the difference in professional soccer and professional football in the United States.

KEY TAKEAWAYS:

- American football, rugby football, and association football all developed in the mid to late 1800s.

13 Billy Perigo, "Why Do Americans Call It Soccer Instead of Football? Blame England," *Time*, July 11, 2018.

- American football, rugby football, and association football were first played at the university level and then expanded from there.
- The FA or Football Association, which oversees the game in England, was founded in 1863 in London by a group of university students.

CHAPTER 2

CONTINUED HISTORY IN ENGLAND AND THE FORMING OF THE FOOTBALL LEAGUE

Just before the founding of the FA in 1863, the first club teams were founded in England. Sheffield FC—which currently resides within conference football (The football leagues below the four professional football leagues) in England—was founded in 1857.[14] They were soon followed by a couple of other clubs, some of which are higher up the tier, including Notts County FC and Stoke City FC.[15]

The development of clubs was followed by the development of The Football League in 1888, only twenty-five years after the standardization of the game. The Football

14 "Football Pioneers," Sheffield F.C., accessed July 3, 2020.

15 "About us," Notts County Football Club, accessed July 3, 2020; "The Story," Stoke City FC, accessed July 3, 2020.

League—William McGregor's Brainchild—was officially announced in London in March 1888.[16] Its efforts supplied the first-ever organized football league, including Accrington, Aston Villa, Blackburn Rovers, Bolton Wanderers, Burnley, Derby County, Everton, Notts County, Preston North End, Stoke, West Bromwich Albion, and Wolverhampton Wanderers.[17]

The initial formation of the league comprising these twelve teams featured two games against each opponent—an away leg and a home leg. The initial point system awarded two points to a team for a win, one point to a team for a draw, and zero points to a team for a loss.[18]

The first season of the league resulted in Preston North End dominating the league with an impressive undefeated season and an eleven-point margin between itself and second-placed Aston Villa while receiving forty out of forty-four possible points.[19]

---

16 "The History of the Football League," The Football League, accessed July 3, 2020.

17 Jamie Ward, "The Founding Clubs of the English Football League: Where Are They Now?" *Bleacher Report*, December 29, 2008.

18 "Final Table for Season 1888-89," English Football League Tables, accessed July 3, 2020.

19 Ibid.

Pos	Team	Pld	W	D	L	GF	GA	GR	Pts	Qualification or relegation
1	Preston North End	22	18	4	0	74	15	4.933	**40**	League Champions and FA Cup Winners
2	Aston Villa	22	12	5	5	61	43	1.419	**29**	
3	Wolverhampton Wanderers	22	12	4	6	51	37	1.378	**28**	
4	Blackburn Rovers	22	10	6	6	66	45	1.467	**26**	
5	Bolton Wanderers	22	10	2	10	63	59	1.068	**22**	
6	West Bromwich Albion	22	10	2	10	40	46	0.870	**22**	
7	Accrington	22	6	8	8	48	48	1.000	**20**	
8	Everton	22	9	2	11	35	47	0.745	**20**	
9	Burnley	22	7	3	12	42	62	0.677	**17**	Re-elected
10	Derby County	22	7	2	13	41	61	0.672	**16**	
11	Notts County	22	5	2	15	40	73	0.548	**12**	
12	Stoke	22	4	4	14	26	51	0.510	**12**	

1888/89 League Table

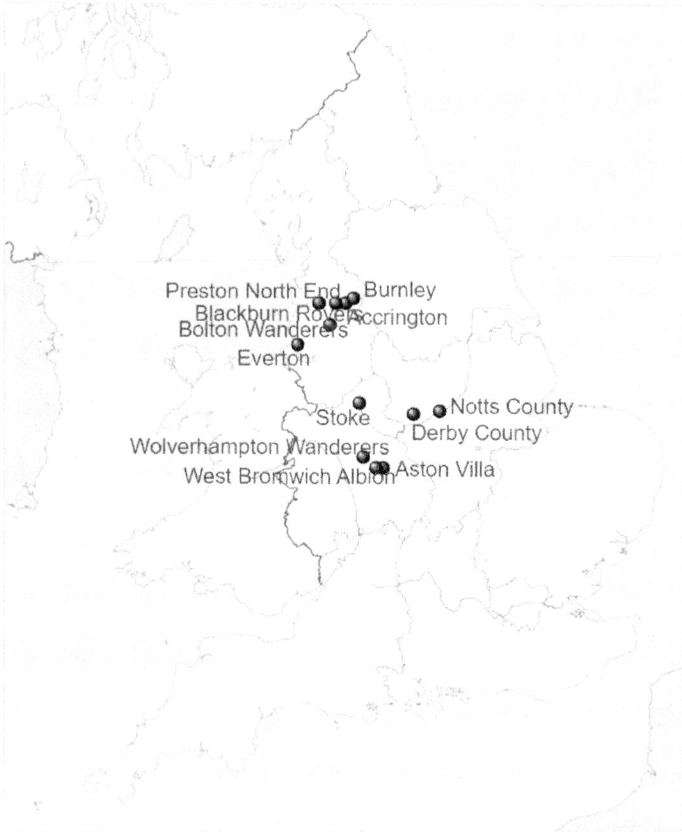

Map of 1888/89 League Teams

The early league also involved a concept known as re-election, which was essentially being chosen—or "elected"—to participate in the league the following season after a finish in the bottom four of the Football League. As teams developed in skill, the makeup of the football league was increased to sixteen teams as more teams strove for election.[20]

After a few years, however, and the introduction of the second division of the football league in the 1892–93 season the concept of relegation was created. This resulted in the lowest teams from the first division being dropped to the second tier while the highest teams from the second tier were added to the first division. Darwen, which was not re-elected after the 1891–92 season, was elected into the newly introduced second division, which made the team the first relegated within the football league, meaning they dropped from one level of the game to the level or tier directly below.[21]

By 1906, there were forty teams in the Football League. Both the top and second division were made up of twenty teams, while only two teams were relegated every season out of the first division and the second division still faced the re-election process following a poor finish in the league. Five of the modern top six teams had already made their way into the football league. The likes of Liverpool, Manchester City, and Arsenal—which were known as Woolwich Arsenal at the time—were already in the top division while Chelsea and Manchester United had both achieved a high finish in the second division that year.[22]

---

20 Roy Emanuel, "How the Re-election Process Shaped the History of the Football League," *Football Chronicle*, August 13, 2018.

21 "Final Table for Season 1892-93," English Football League Tables, accessed July 3, 2020; "Final Table for Season 1891-92," English Football League Tables, accessed July 3, 2020.

22 "Final Table for Season 1905-06," English Football League Tables, accessed July 3, 2020.

Tottenham Hotspur, however, was nowhere to be seen after a total of three games during the 1905–06 season, all taking place within the FA Cup, the biggest Domestic Cup in England that runs concurrently with the league system.[23] Not until the 1908–09 season did Spurs make their league debut in which they achieved promotion into the top tier of English Football on the first opportunity.[24]

***

The FA Cup is the biggest domestic cup in England. The difference between a domestic cup and a domestic league is that the cup competition is between several clubs all from the same domestic system that compete in a series of knockout rounds until one team remains. A domestic league, on the other hand, is a league competition meaning it involves a set number of teams from the same level in a domestic system, i.e. The English Premier League. The teams face off against each other over the course of the season accumulating points based on results. At the end of the season, the team with the most points wins the season outright. While neither competition directly impacts the other one, domestic cups and domestic leagues generally run at the same time.

The demarcation as a domestic cup is necessary because many teams that compete at the highest level in their home country also participate in a third kind of competition during the same season. This is known as a continental competition depending upon the other teams involved. The UEFA

---

23 Ibid.

24 "Final Table for Season 1908-09," English Football League Tables, accessed July 3, 2020.

Champions League, for example, includes teams from across Europe based on their performance in the previous season, either within the domestic league or domestic cup of their respective nation.

Another form of competition, known as an international competition, takes place between different football associations such as the English FA and U.S. Soccer in which the national teams from both countries would compete. The World Cup, the European Championship, and the Gold Cup are examples of this kind of competition.

***

In 1919–20, the FA expanded the leagues once again to a total of forty-four teams across the two divisions, with twenty-two in each. This was also the first season that Arsenal appeared as Arsenal rather than Woolwich Arsenal.[25]

During the following 1920–21 season, an additional third division was created. The first two leagues had been based primarily in the Midlands with a few teams from farther north, such as Newcastle United or Sunderland, and a few teams from the south, especially from London, such as Fulham, Chelsea, Arsenal, or Tottenham Hotspur. However, the new third division was composed exclusively of southern teams, including a few London clubs, such as Crystal Palace, Millwall, and Watford. Many south coast teams also joined the league after the region's league status had been neglected,

---

25 "Final Table for Season 1919-20," English Football League Tables, accessed July 3, 2020.

such as Southampton, Brighton & Hove Albion, and Portsmouth. Grimsby Town was the team located farthest north during the inaugural season after being relegated from the second division the previous year.[26]

The following season, the league expanded once again, but instead of adding a division to the bottom of the pyramid, another third division was added. The resulting league structure featured the two original twenty-two team leagues on top of two joint third-tier leagues, the Third Division North comprised twenty teams, but by the 1923–24 season there were twenty-two teams, and the Third Division South comprised twenty-two teams.[27]

The Football League split at that level because the lower league teams of the north and south could not afford to travel up and down the country for various league games all the time. The new system decreased the operating price of the league and localized the sport, giving fans more opportunities to see their club on the road and more chances to play local rivals.

As in America today, travel costs for smaller clubs are significant deterrents to the development and organization of leagues in lower-tier soccer, hence why many American sports teams, especially those competing in leagues below the top division of their sport, participate in regional or local leagues. In fact, geography poses a much bigger obstacle

26 "Final Table for Season 1920-21," English Football League Tables, accessed July 3, 2020.

27 "Final Table for Season 1921-22," English Football League Tables, accessed July 3, 2020.

in modern America than it did in England a century ago, despite the technological developments since then.

KEY TAKEAWAYS:

- It took almost sixty years to get from the founding of the first club to the creation of four leagues, which is the current number of professional leagues in the English system.
- As the quality and organization of teams increased, so too did the size of the league.
- The leagues were founded with the principles of promotion and relegation as an integral part of stimulating the fluidity and growth of the game.
- The spread of the Football League was partially geographic, leaving the portion of the country south of London for last.
- America faces a huge geographical obstacle.

Map of Other Teams Mentioned

CHAPTER 3

THE BEGINNING IN AMERICA

Another tremendous soccer-related event occurred in 1921. Thomas Cahill, the father of American soccer, met with eight teams and established the American Soccer League (ASL).[28]

The newly established league, in union with the United States Football Association (USFA), exploded with tremendous potential building on the history of the sport being played at colleges across the country. Relying on immigrants as fans and players, the popularity of the league was rivaled only by that of professional baseball as thousands of fans showed up to every game.[29]

28 Christopher Klein, "The Forgotten Age of American Soccer: As the World Cup sparks soccer fever around the world, look back at the forgotten golden age of American soccer—the 1920s," *History*, updated August 22, 2018.

29 Ibid.

Teams even received corporate sponsorships from big local businesses that had developed in the wake of the American Civil War during the Gilded Age. One such sponsorship was from Charles Schwab. The businesses would employ worker-players who would perform on the pitch as well as within the factory. Local heroes like Billy Gonsalves and Bert Patenaude were also created as they led their local teams to domestic success.[30]

The United States was even poised to succeed at the international level through the 1930 World Cup in Uruguay, when the Americans received two consecutive 3–0 victories over Belgium and Paraguay, before being thumped 6–1 by Argentina in the semifinal. Patenaude and Gonsalves, however, thrived on the big stage as they led the United States to their first and best finish in the World Cup to this day, finishing in third place behind the Argentinian runners-up and the Uruguayan hosts.[31]

Despite initial successes and popularity, the ASL was not to last. The big business sponsors who provided promising work were steadily tempting immigrant talent away from Europe. Many Europeans were fed up with the Americans tempting their players away despite the existence of binding contracts. After FIFA threatened to kick the Americans out of world football, they agreed on terms involving transfer regulations to prevent further corruption by the U.S. corporations.[32]

---

30 Ibid.

31 "Hosts Uruguay beat arch-rivals to first world crown," FIFA.com, March 22, 2007.

32 Klein, "The Forgotten Age of American Soccer."

FIFA's frustration in tandem with the Immigration Act of 1924 by the United States Government proved a fatal blow to the league. The USFA and the ASL also disagreed over whether teams should be required to participate in the domestic cup, now known as the U.S. Open Cup. The ASL chose to boycott the tournament, and after a few teams refused to boycott, they were expelled from the league.[33]

Upon learning of their expulsion, FIFA and the ASL began to fight over the legality of the move. Eventually, FIFA convicted them as an "Outlaw League." Then in October 1929, the stock market plummeted, and corporations were forced to pull funding from the ASL. These hardships caused the league to sputter to a halt before dissociating in 1933.[34]

The power struggle between the USFA and ASL combined with the interference by FIFA in the late twenties was disastrous for the sport. What Americans dubbed "The Soccer Wars" was so difficult for fans to ignore that they began to avoid the sport altogether in an effort to forget about the corruption.[35] Despite steps taken throughout the twenties, there was no major organized American soccer league in the U.S. until after the end of World War II.

***

Other American sports, on the other hand, did not fail.

---

33 Ibid.

34 Ibid.

35 Ibid.

The 1920s have been marked as the golden age of American sports. The Bull Economy of the majority of the 1920s made it possible for the middle class to not only grow but also enjoy a fairly comfortable life, which included the introduction of a new class of fans.

Baseball was the most popular sport, and this period led to the sport's nickname as America's national pastime. Babe Ruth, perhaps the most famous baseball player of all time, also had his rise to fame during this period with the Boston Red Sox and the New York Yankees.[36]

The era of pre-depression prosperity made it possible for fandom to increase and spread. This increase led to a much higher level of public interest in sports and an overall higher social value on athletic institutions such as professional football or baseball.

***

While soccer stalled in the late twenties with corruption and interference, other sports took off and dominated the sporting industry, leaving no room for soccer. Had the sport been given the chance to continue and develop, American soccer would be a completely different beast than it is today. The country would be only a couple of decades behind the English and their model system, rather than almost a century. Had the league been given the chance to grow, there is no telling what heights they would have reached.

36 Ibid.

The seventy extra years of development that the ASL would have on Major League Soccer are irreplaceable. The nation missed a prime opportunity to get into the game while the stakes were so much lower. The level of catch-up now required to achieve similar levels of success as the top European leagues is tremendous.

American soccer must spend both a formidable amount of money and time to develop the leagues to the point they would have been had they kept the league afloat a century ago.

Not only would the league be competitive among other leagues in the soccer industry, but they would also be a much greater contender within the American sports industry. Had the league held on, they would have timelines to rival the NFL, MLB, NHL, and NBA and would have a much more established standing among those leagues, bringing the national popularity and participation in the sport to much greater levels.

KEY TAKEAWAYS:

- The first effort to begin an American Soccer League accompanied the growth of many other sports leagues in the 1920s.
- The United States did well at the first World Cup.
- Corruption and scandal brought down the first attempt at an American Soccer League.
- Had the league survived, the sport would be much more competitive in the United States with other domestic sports and with rival soccer leagues abroad.

CHAPTER 4

UEFA COMPETITION AND CONTINENTAL SUCCESS

UEFA, or the Union of European Football Associations, held their first-ever intercontinental competition during the 1955–56 season, which was known as the European Cup and was an ancestor of what has evolved into the UEFA Champions League. Initially, the competition consisted of sixteen teams from sixteen different countries from around Europe, and these sixteen clubs were selected by the French Magazine *L'equipe* for the first five years of the competition.[37]

The first season included Rapid Vien from Vienna, Austria; RSC Anderlecht from Brussels, Belgium; AGF Aarhus from Aarhus, Denmark; Stade de Reims from Reims, France; Vörös Lobogó, now known as MTK Budapest FC from Budapest, Hungary; AC Milan from Milan, Italy; PSV Eindhoven from

37 "1955/56: Madrid Claim First Crown," UEFA Champions League, updated September 27, 2014.

Eindhoven, Netherlands; Gwardia Warszawa from Warsaw, Poland; Sporting CP from Lisbon, Portugal; FC Saarbrucken from Saarbrucken, Saarland—which became part of the nation of West Germany the following year; Hibernian FC from Edinburgh, Scotland; Real Madrid from Madrid, Spain; Djurgardens IF from the Swedish Island of Djurgarden; Servette FC from Geneva, Switzerland; Rot-Weiss Essen from Essen, Germany; and Partizan Belgrade from Belgrade, Yugoslavia.[38]

Map of Teams from 1955/56 Season

38 "1955/56 Season: Madrid win first edition," UEFA Champions League, accessed July 6, 2020.

After four stages of the competition, featuring a home and an away leg in each round, up until the final, one team remained to claim the title of Champion of Europe—Real Madrid outlasted Stade de Reims in a 4–3 victory in Paris in 1956.[39] This was the first time European clubs had competed for continental success rather than solely domestic, and it would change the terrain of world football irreversibly.

The following season, the competition, which had been a success around Europe, exploded with excitement. Six additional countries sought glory through success in the European Cup, including Bulgaria, Czechoslovakia, England, Luxembourg, Romania, and Turkey. Spain also entered a new challenger to the defending Real Madrid as their national champion as *Los Blancos* sought to repeat their victory. Except for Saarland, every country chose to continue participation.[40] The Central European Nation was no longer eligible to enter a team, having reunited into West Germany that year.[41]

There were twenty-two teams, which any college basketball fan could tell you won't make an even bracket. To fix this problem, they developed a new system for the season. They sorted the teams into two categories, those who were defending champions: population one, and those who were not: population twenty-one. The twenty-one challengers were placed in a pool and twelve names were chosen. These twelve teams were set to face off against another from the twelve in the first-ever European Cup qualifying round. After these

39 Ibid.

40 "1956/57 Season: Madrid champions again at the Bernabéu," UEFA Champions League, accessed July 6, 2020.

41 *Encyclopaedia Britannica Online*, s.v. "Saarland," accessed July 6, 2020.

games had been played, sixteen teams remained, and they played their standard four-stage knockout tournament. Real Madrid once again was the last one standing and defended their title.[42]

During the 1957–58 season, the European Cup consisted of twenty-four teams, with twenty-three clubs in the pool eligible for preliminary rounds. The newly represented countries were the Republic of Ireland, Northern Ireland, and East Germany. Spain sent an additional team again due to the failure of the Turkish Football Association to register Besiktas. Real Madrid once again defended their domination of the continent.[43] The following season, two more countries received representation; Greece and Finland both sent their champion to the tournament for the first time. Spain once again received an additional spot, and England received two teams for the first time.[44]

Despite the twenty-eight teams registered for the tournament, only twenty-six participated.[45] Manchester United, one of the English delegates, was still traumatized from losing eight of their players to the Munich Air Disaster the previous season.[46] Olympiakos, the first Greek representatives, refused to participate for geopolitical reasons after drawing the Turkish

---

42 "1956/57: Gento doubles up for Madrid," UEFA Champions League, updated September 27, 2014.

43 "1957/58 Season: Madrid claim third consecutive title in Brussels," UEFA Champions League, accessed July 6, 2020.

44 "1958/59 Season: Mateo's early strike helps Madrid to fourth cup victory," UEFA Champions League, accessed July 6, 2020.

45 Ibid.

46 "Munich Air Disaster: The survivors who never played again," *Sky News*, February 6, 2018.

side Besiktas from Istanbul.[47] The next season featured twenty-seven teams as Spain once again received an additional bid due to Madrid's continued success. Upon the draw, however, the Finnish club, Kuopion Palloseura, withdrew.[48]

The twenty-six remaining teams participated in the preliminary round, narrowing down the field to sixteen, only for Real Madrid to walk the league once again, scoring an astounding seven goals in the final against Eintracht Frankfurt.[49] The 1960–61 competition was the first time a Norwegian Club participated and the first time Benfica, or any club besides Real Madrid, won the competition.[50] By the 1967–68 season, the cup had expanded to thirty-two teams and had club representatives from the USSR, Iceland, Cyprus, Albania, and Malta. This also meant that the preliminary round had shrunk, and that all thirty-two teams played a game in the first of five rounds of bracket-style play.[51]

***

On February 6, 1958, the world was left in shock by the tragedy of the Munich Air Disaster. On their way back to England from a European Cup match in Yugoslavia against Red Star Belgrade, the plane carrying Manchester United

---

47 *Encyclopaedia Britannica Online*, s.v., "EOKA," accessed July 6, 2020.

48 "1959/60 Season: Madrid lift cup after ten-goal thriller," UEFA Champions League, accessed July 6, 2020.

49 "1959/60: Dazzling Madrid crush Frankfurt," UEFA Champions League, updated September 27, 2014.

50 "1960/61 Season: Benfica become first Portuguese Trophy Winners," UEFA Champions League, accessed July 6, 2020.

51 "1967/68 Season: United soar in extra time to overcome Benfica," UEFA Champions League, accessed July 6, 2020.

players and staff, as well as reporters and other passengers, tragically crashed while attempting to take off in Munich, taking the lives of twenty-three people in all, including eight of United's players.[52]

The event marked one of the most tragic in the world of football and set the context for Manchester United passing up the opportunity to participate in the upcoming 1958–59 European Cup.

***

At the same time during the late 1950s, there was turmoil in southeastern Europe. Greece and Turkey were caught in a heated debate over the future of the island Cyprus. The Greek Cypriots were in support of the EOKA (Ethniki Organosis Kyprion Agoniston or National Organization of Cypriot Fighters), an insurgent group of the majority Greek-Cypriots who were in conflict with the minority Turkish-Cypriots, who also occupied the island. The British government, which controlled Cyprus as a colony, backed the Turkish side.[53]

The geopolitical circumstances relating to Cyprus and the Greece-Turkey conflict on the island was the context behind Olympiakos and their refusal to travel to an away game in Istanbul.

***

52 "Munich Air Disaster.

53 Encyclopedia Britannica Online, s.v., "Saarland."

The UEFA European Cup was essential in the collective growth of the game not only for European leagues but also for their national teams that became more accustomed to the idea of a continental competition pinning them against players of other countries and nationalities.

The UEFA European Cup also made for a competition that required more traveling than had ever been needed to play the sport. It's no coincidence that European football didn't take off until after airplanes became a common form of transportation. From Lisbon to Moscow, it's 4557 kilometers or 2832 miles.[54] From Oslo to Istanbul, it's 3213 kilometers, or 1996 miles.[55] For comparison, the longest travel distance in English football from Bournemouth to Newcastle is about 563 kilometers, or 350 miles, in other words, about one-eighth or roughly 12 percent of the distance from Lisbon to Moscow.[56] Germany's longest distance—Freiberg to Berlin—clocks in at 809 kilometers or 502 miles, or 18 percent.[57] France's Brest to Monaco comes in at 1460 kilometers or 907 miles, or 32 percent.[58]

While the distances in domestic leagues can grow like that of Monaco and Brest, on opposite corners of France, the

---

54 "Directions for Driving from Moscow, Russia to Lisbon, Portugal," Google Maps, accessed July 6, 2020.

55 "Directions for Driving from Oslo, Norway to Istanbul, Turkey," Google Maps, accessed July 6, 2020.

56 "Directions for Driving from Bournemouth, United Kingdom to Newcastle upon Tyne, United Kingdom," Google Maps, accessed July 6, 2020.

57 "Directions for Driving from Freiburg im Breisgau, Germany to Berlin, Germany," Google Maps, accessed July 6, 2020.

58 "Directions for Driving from Brest, France to Monaco City, Monaco," Google Maps, accessed July 6, 2020.

level of travel in European football across countries was much more substantial, having the longest matchup more than three times the length of the farthest necessary fixture travel in France, England, or Germany.

Oslo to Istanbul

Moscow to Lisbon

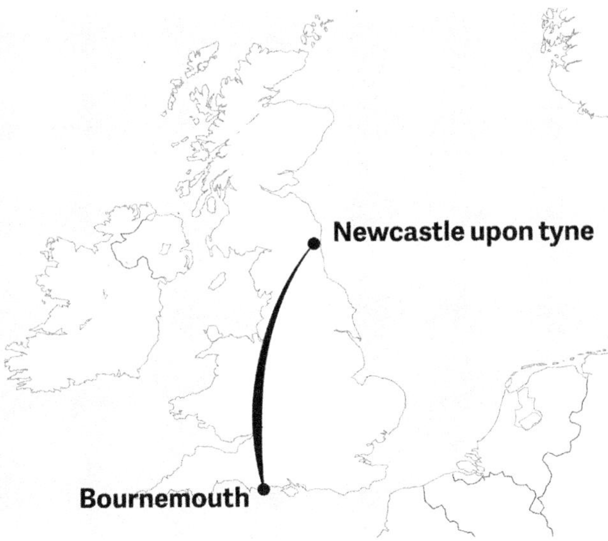

Newcastle-upon-Tyne to Bournemouth

Berlin to Freiberg im Breisgau

Brest to Monaco

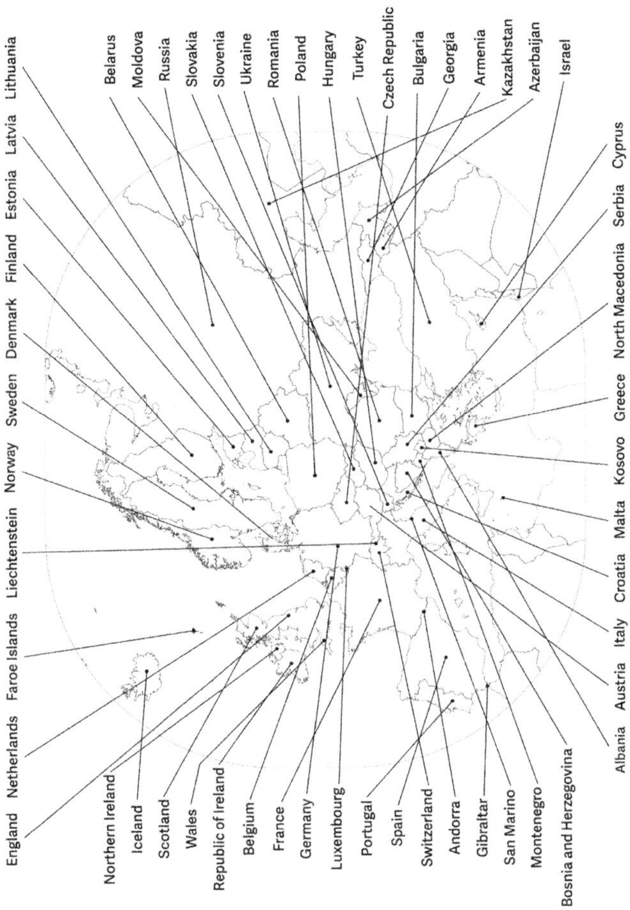

Current Nations Eligible for UEFA Competitions

CHAPTER 5

LEADING UP TO THE BIGGEST YEAR IN FOOTBALL

In England, after the 1957–58 season, the bottom twelve of the Third Division North and the Third Division South, which had both been expanded to twenty-four teams on the back of the 1948–49 season, were moved to the newly integrated fourth division while places 2–12 were moved to the newly redesigned Third Division along with the two bottom finishers of the Second Division.[59]

The new system featured the original two upper divisions operating the same way while the Third Division was now a single league of twenty-four teams with four relegation spots at the bottom of the table. The Fourth Division featured

59 "Final Table for Season 1958/59," English Football league Tables, accessed July 6, 2020.

twenty-four more teams with four promotion spots at the top and four re-election spots at the bottom end of the table.[60]

***

In the United States on the other hand, after the failure of the ASL in the 1930s, soccer would have a major decline over the next thirty years. The sport had been relegated to an amateur sport for which there was no professional league system. In the 1960s, however, two separate leagues materialized within the United States.[61]

The United Soccer Association, or USA, was sanctioned by FIFA and began as clubs from around the world, specifically, European and South American clubs imported teams. The National Professional Soccer League, or NPSL, was also founded in 1967 with the first-ever American soccer television contract. After trouble for both leagues, they combined to form the North American Soccer League, or NASL, which consisted of clubs from both leagues.[62]

Television contracts are crucial to the success of a league and its teams. Without contracts like the ones American sports have, in which big TV channels pay the league a large sum for the rights to air the games, the league (and the teams) would be deprived of a lot of revenue and the sports industry would not be anywhere near as lucrative.

---

60 Ibid.

61 Michael McDuffie, "The Strange Story of the United Soccer Association," *PunditFeed*, May 4, 2020.

62 Ibid.

The newly founded NASL provided a series of glory years for American soccer, attracting the likes of Pelé, Johann Cruyff, Franz Beckenbauer, George Best, Bobby Moore, and many more impressive footballers. This attraction of world talents in their declining years draws parallels to Steven Gerard and Zlatan Ibrahimovic moving to Major League Soccer over the last couple of years.[63]

The NASL was the second attempt in the history of soccer in America to start a league with the backing of funding, resources, and community support. America struggled to create a league that would flourish in the untapped market that was the rich, ethnically diverse, and modern United States.

The NASL invented their own system of compiling a league table that many would question. Their new system was not only reliant on whether the teams won, drew, or lost but also relied on the number of goals scored by each team. Teams received an astonishing six points for a win, three points for a draw, zero points for a loss, and one point for every goal scored—with a maximum of three points possible from that method.[64]

While some might call this novel system absurd or impractical, it was actually a good idea because the rules encouraged more attacking play. Attacking play leads to more goals and goal-scoring opportunities, which help build support and interest from a community of fans who may not have grown

63 "NASL 1968-84: A review of the Golden Era," NASL, accessed July 6, 2020.

64 Ibid,

up playing or watching soccer. After all, many Americans' main complaint about the game is that there are very few scores and it's not exciting enough. In fact, throughout the existence of the league, the league averaged about 3.27 goals per game, while the English Premier League up to the 2013–14 season averaged only about 2.62 goals, more than half a goal less per game.[65]

The NASL scoring system also discouraged "cynical play"—or play that encouraged a physical, low-scoring style of play. For example, this cynical game has been popularized recently by Jose Mourinho, the current manager of Tottenham Hotspur and the ex-manager of Manchester United and Chelsea. Mourinho has developed a reputation for parking the Bus—or playing with an ultra-defensive formation with the defenders and some midfielders staying back on attacks and maintaining a defensive shield—in the hopes of keeping a clean sheet and potentially drawing a goal from a counter-attack. Such tactics lead to little exciting play by either team and often result in 0–0, or 1–0 scorelines.

They also introduced the American idea of having divisions based upon geography within the same league, even modern Major League Soccer features an eastern and western division to reduce travel costs of teams participating.[66] This hearkens back to when the English Football Association had divided leagues to reduce travel costs for lower league teams. The only difference is the American conferences were divided yet still within the same league as they played each other in

65 "North American Soccer League," SoccerStats.us, accessed July 6, 2020; "Premier League," SoccerStats.us, accessed July 6, 2020.

66 "NASL 1968-84," NASL.

league matches throughout the season. They just tended to populate their schedules more densely with teams from their own geographic conference.

***

The final big American idea still present in Major League Soccer is the idea of a playoff to determine the winner of a season.[67] Many European leagues, including England, the primary example within this timeline, also feature playoffs, but they are primarily used to spark further competition over a single promotion place into a higher league for teams not quite able to clinch a high enough finish in the league table for automatic promotion. They are also featured in cup competitions played completely separately from league competitions, in which the results do not affect each other.

For example, the Championship (England's second tier) promotes three teams each season to replace the three teams relegated from the Premier League. The first- and second-placed teams both achieve what is called automatic promotion. The third team, however, is decided by a playoff between the four clubs finishing third through sixth.

This is done not only to stimulate fandom through playing more games but also to shrink the tedium of the mid-table. While many clubs would be happy finishing midtable in the Championship, having a larger range for potential promotion leads to much more excitement being generated throughout the season. Instead of having to push for third, many clubs

---

67 Ibid.

are satisfied with a ninth or tenth place position that leaves them within striking position of the sixth place cut off for promotion playoffs. This, overall, creates a lot more excitement throughout a season than a single automatic spot would.

Many European Football Associations also feature a winner-take-all bracketed domestic cup competition such as the FA Cup. The recently renamed Carabao Cup is another example. They are both multi-league competitions in England that feature over ninety teams and give lower league teams a chance to upset the premier league highflyers as they attempt to avoid embarrassment.

The American playoff is different from these. After the finish of the regular season in most American sports, the best teams are awarded specific seeds or spots on a predetermined bracket. This bracket, whether it be sixty-eight teams like the NCAA basketball tournament or the four-team NCAA football playoff, then plays through the bracket with a series of elimination games in which the loser goes home and the winner continues to the next round until one team remains to claim the title for the entire season. This means that the winner of the league has very little, if anything, to do with the winner of the regular season.

While American playoffs do build more ambiguity and romance than a league like the Premier league would, they fail to reward the outright winners of the league for their consistent success.

***

The NASL playoffs consisted of the top teams from all four conferences facing off in a four-team bracket. The teams then played a home and an away leg against their selected opponent and the winners on aggregate score advanced to the finals dubbed the Soccer Bowl, which also consisted of home and away legs where the winner was once again determined based upon aggregate score.[68]

In 1968, after the first season consisting of seventeen teams and four conferences, a whopping twelve teams folded, leaving only five teams to play in the second season of the NASL. The Kansas City Spurs, Atlanta Chiefs, Dallas Tornado, Saint Louis Stars, and Baltimore Bays were the only remaining teams within the league.[69]

A few factors were involved, but the common variable across them all was money. Many investors pulled funding for their various teams because the first season was not profitable, and they decided it would be best to cut their losses and end their teams. The first season failed on a variety of fields. There were not enough quality domestic players to field a team of entirely or even mostly American players, and foreign players were expensive. This left owners choosing between affordability or skill. That problem was magnified by the fact that attendance was much lower than they would have liked.[70]

If the teams were financially conservative, quality would suffer, and the team would lose more revenue from even lower

---

68 Ibid.

69 "North American Soccer League: 1969," SoccerStats.us, accessed July 6, 2020.

70 NASL 1968-84," NASL.

attendance. If they decided to cash in on more expensive players, they would cost much more, and given the already low attendance, the investors would have to pay out of their own pockets to afford such skill.

The situation worsened even further when CBS pulled out of the television contract agreed upon a year earlier.[71]

The league needed business improvement to survive.

As the league steadily regrew, they lost the Kansas City Spurs, one of the veteran teams, but the league managed to rebound from the dangerous dip by increasing attendance. By the 1975 season, the NASL had twenty teams playing again. The league hit its stride in the late seventies and early eighties as the New York Cosmos, the team that acquired Pelé, raised the popularity of the league. Over seventy thousand people showed up in New York to watch them play multiple times during the league's glory days. The average attendance, however, was much lower than that, clocking in around twenty-eight thousand.[72]

For the sake of comparison, the average New York Cosmos attendance rivals the English Football League teams Newcastle's and Chelsea's thirty-eight thousand and forty-three thousand respective average attendance games of the 1919–20 season roughly fifty years previously.[73]

---

71 Ibid.

72 Ibid.

73 "Game Attendance Summary for Season 1919-20: Average League Gate Home and Away," English Football League Tables, accessed July 6, 2020.

By 1982, however, the league had dropped back down to fourteen teams from the high of twenty-four just two seasons ago. Having lost ten teams in the last two seasons, the NASL was doomed. The following season, only twelve teams participated, and in 1985 after losing another three teams, the league folded completely and the second attempt at a self-sufficient American league for soccer failed.[74]

***

Ironically, the failure of the NASL stemmed from over-expansion, a problem they would have readily welcomed eighteen years earlier. Clive Toye, the former owner of the New York Cosmos, told Michael Lewis in an interview with *The Guardian* in 2018, "We had a league meeting and a group of us decided we had to get rid of six of those eighteen [clubs] because they were rubbish and we were better to progress with the twelve decent ones, which included people like [Chicago owner] Lee Stern and Lamar Hunt...We went to a meeting. The New York mob ... and some of the idiots said: 'We must expand and not diminish, and we must add them, them, them, them' because we had people applying willing to pay $2 million a franchise. That was the beginning of the decline of the NASL as an entity."[75]

The NASL, however, was not a failure. Toye told Lewis in the same interview that "the NASL as a crusader was a magnificent success. As a business, it eventually failed as a single entity. But it left behind a knowledge of the game that didn't

74 "NASL 1968-84," NASL.

75 Michael Lewis, "How the birth and death of the NASL changed soccer in America forever," *The Guardian*, October 20, 2018.

even exist in this country before and enthusiasm for the game which never existed before."[76]

Toye's point is a good one. The league managed to bring in some of the top players of the era, from Pelé to Bobby Moore. They were the first American soccer league to ever receive television coverage. In 1973 a soccer player appeared on the cover of *Sports Illustrated* for the first time. The crowning achievement was that in 1988, four years after the folding of the league, the United States managed to win the bid for the 1994 FIFA World Cup.

Without the founding of the NASL, the United States never would have rediscovered soccer. They never would have set the precedent necessary for the founding of Major League Soccer a decade later. They never would have had an opportunity to host the World Cup and bring the best soccer players of the world to the United States at their peaks. And most importantly, they never would have developed a series of successful women's World Cup squads, with the women winning the competition twice in the 1990s, and a successful 2002 men's team.[77]

---

76 Ibid.

77 "World Cup Women: Archive," FlashScore.com, accessed July 6, 2020; World Cup 2002: Summary." FlashScore.com, accessed July 6, 2020.

KEY TAKEAWAYS:

- The NASL was the second attempt to build a soccer league in the United States.
- While the NASL came to an end, it was not a complete failure, as it set the precedent for American soccer down the line.
- The seventies were an extremely formative decade in the history of American soccer.

CHAPTER 6

1993

The 1992–93 season was a big one in world football. Both the English Football League (EFL) and the European Cup were rebranded. The top division of the EFL became the Premier League while the following division became known as the Championship, League One and League Two.[78] The newly named Divisions two through four did however remain part of the EFL, just with new names, as the Premier League distinguished itself as separate from the EFL.

The promotion-relegation relationship between the leagues remained the same, however, except for the playoff system, which shifted from the first three teams to miss promotion and the last team to avoid relegation to just the four top teams to miss promotion, while one more relegation spot was added to the league.

In the same year, the European Cup was rebranded as the Champions League. The new Champions League awarded participation to completely new nations, including Estonia,

78 "1992/93 Season Review," Premier League, accessed July 6, 2020.

Faroe Islands, Israel, Slovenia, Latvia, Ukraine, Lithuania, and Russia.[79] Many of these participants were newly formed countries that arose after the USSR dissolved in December 1991.

The Champions League also integrated a new system that had been tested the previous year. After two rounds, the field of thirty-two teams was narrowed down to eight teams. The remaining teams were then sorted into two groups of four and played a home and an away match against the other three teams in their group. At the end of the group stage, the team with the most points from each group would face off in the Champions League final at a predetermined neutral location—a single match that would decide the winner of the Tournament.[80]

***

1993 was also a big year for American soccer. In preparation for hosting the 1994 World Cup, the U.S., along with a few investors who will be discussed in the next chapter, began their third, most recent, and most successful attempt thus far to tap into the United States for soccer potential. While work began on MLS in 1993, the league didn't kick off its first season until 1996.[81]

The three big shifts in 1993 represent the transition from one chapter of soccer to another. The widespread

79 "1992/93 Season: French first in Inaugural Champions League season," UEFA Champions League, accessed July 6, 2020.

80 Ibid.

81 FRASER v. MAJOR LEAGUE SOCCER, 284 F.3d 47, (1st Cir. 2002).

commercialization and rebranding of both the Champions League and the Premier League perfectly represent the shift from the game being played for the sake of the game to the new financial incentive to the industry. There was money in the sport before 1993, but the culmination of that trend with the new brands finalized that shift, leading to an immense wealth gap between the top clubs of Europe and England, and the other clubs below them.

The shift also explains why within the Premier League since the inaugural season in 1992–93, only seven teams have won the league, including Blackburn Rovers (1994–95); Manchester United (1992–93, 1993–94, 1995–96, 1996–97, 1998–99, 1999–00, 2000–01, 2002–03, 2006–07, 2007–08, 2008–09, 2010–11, 2012–13); Arsenal (1997–98, 2001–02, 2003–04); Chelsea (2004–05, 2005–06, 2009–10, 2014–15, 2016–17); Manchester City (2011–12, 2013–14, 2017–18, 2018–19); Leicester City (2015–16); and Liverpool most recently in the 2019–20 season. Five of the seven teams come from the six richest clubs in English football, with four of them being the only clubs to have won the league multiple times since the rebrand in the nineties.[82]

With the overall rebranding also came a series of uber-wealthy investors making those clubs into the richest clubs. Stan Kroenke of Arsenal, Roman Abromovich of Chelsea, and Sheikh Mansour of Manchester City are just a few examples.[83]

---

82 "English Football Final League Tables," English Football League Tables, accessed July 6, 2020; "Tables: First Team," Premier League, accessed July 6, 2020.

83 Josh Fordham, "LOADED Newcastle Takeover: Where Saudi group will rank on Premier League rich list alongside Man City and Chelsea's billionaire owners," *talkSPORT*, May 21, 2020.

While many clubs have their own version of these investors, these three men have been some of the most transformative in the history of their respective clubs, the English league, and the game as a whole.

News of the most recent and most well-funded example broke during the Covid-19 pandemic in Spring 2020—the takeover of Newcastle United by the Crown Prince of Saudi Arabia, Mohammed bin Salman. The Saudi Arabia Public Investment Fund he chairs has an estimated £260 billion. This is almost ten times that of Sheikh Mansour, previously the wealthiest owner, and his operation at Manchester City.[84]

This is the same Saudi Arabian government that murdered American journalist Jamal Khashoggi in 2018 under Bin Salman's direct order. In an interview with CNN in the Spring of 2020 after hearing about the takeover, Hatice Cengiz, Khashoggi's fianceé, called for the Premier League to block the move, saying, "Doing otherwise will greatly stain the reputation of the Premier League and the UK. Mohamed Bin Salman is strategically using international sports to repair his badly damaged reputation after the murder of Jamal."[85]

---

84 Ibid.

85 George Ramsay, "Newcastle United takeover will 'greatly stain' Premier League, says Jamal Khashoggi's Fiancée," *CNN.* April 27, 2020.

KEY TAKEAWAYS:

- 1993 marks the transition year from two very different periods of soccer history as well as the beginning of the idea for MLS.
- A lot of success in modern football stems from access to money.

2019/20 English Premier League Teams

2019/20 EFL Championship Teams

2019/20 EFL League One Teams

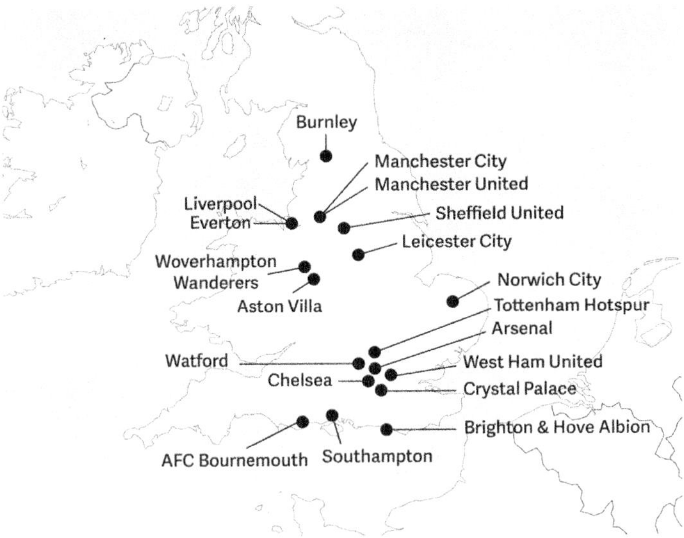

2019/20 EFL League Two Teams

CHAPTER 7

THE START OF MAJOR LEAGUE SOCCER

Major League Soccer needed to succeed.

MLS needed to build a successful American soccer league this time around because there was a very good chance this was America's final opportunity to build a league. To make sure the league was safe, MLS needed to improve the ownership of the newborn clubs that would populate the newly created league. They couldn't take owners like the ones who had nearly destroyed the NASL after a single season by pulling funds.

The key to circumnavigating the ownership obstacles previously faced by American soccer was a different business model. Instead of the model that is commonplace throughout world soccer and American sports, Major League Soccer required investors not buy into teams but into the league itself; they were known as investor-operators. The investor-operators were rewarded for their investment by being permitted to operate a club, hence the operator portion of their title.

Subsequently, the league attracted a few early investors who were the primary funders of the early days of the league.[86] The novel business model made for evenly distributed funds and a solid central governing body, which were very important in avoiding the shortcomings of the NASL. The downside of the league, however, was that due to the diluted ownership of clubs, there was a lack of competitive drive.

The league only received enough investment to support ten teams. The first ten teams in Major League Soccer were Tampa Bay Mutiny, Los Angeles Galaxy, D.C. United, Dallas Burn, Kansas City Wizards, San Jose Clash, New York/New Jersey Metro Stars, Columbus Crew, New England Revolution, and Colorado Rapids.[87] The investor-operator pool during the first season contained very little diversity as Lamar Hunt, an American businessman who made a significant contribution in promoting soccer and founding MLS, owned two out of the ten teams. He initially owned the Kansas City Wizards, who went on to change their name to Sporting Kansas City to conform to a more traditional soccer naming style in 2010. He was also the investor-operator of Columbus Crew.[88]

86 Isaac Krasny, "Unpacking the Major League Soccer Business Model," *Medium*, June 7, 2017.

87 "Major League Soccer: 1996," SoccerStats.us, accessed July 7, 2020.

88 "MLS team owners: Charlotte's David Tepper joins burgeoning list," MLS, December 21, 2019.

1996 MLS Teams

A few teams, specifically Los Angeles Galaxy and D.C. United, were owned not by an individual but by entities within their cities designed to own the club. Los Angeles was started by L.A. Soccer Partners LP, and D.C. was owned by Washington Soccer LP, a foundation funded primarily by George Soros.[89]

The league began three of the remaining six teams to increase the number of teams in the league and to provide more competition for the seven clubs owned by separate investor-operators. Tampa Bay Mutiny, one of very few MLS teams to have failed, was owned by MLS along with Dallas Burn, who eventually evolved into Dallas FC, which was bought by Lamar Hunt in 2001.[90]

89 Ibid.

90 Ibid.

San Jose Crush, which later became the San Jose Earthquakes, was also owned by the league until Robert Kraft, the founding and current investor-operator of the New England Revolution, purchased them following the 1998 season. John Kluge and Stuart Subotnick owned the New York/New Jersey MetroStars upon the founding of the league before unloading the teams onto one of the biggest investor-operators in the league, Anschutz Entertainment Group.[91]

Anschutz Entertainment Group was the final and most invested investor-operator in MLS. One of the biggest sports-owning corporations in the world, they flitted from club to club buying and selling bits and pieces. Throughout the late nineties after the founding of the league and through the 2000s, they owned seven different teams for at least one period. They were the initial investors, however, in the Colorado Rapids team that began MLS in 1996.[92]

They steadily grew and acquired both D.C. United and the Los Angeles Galaxy. They were also the original investors in both the Chicago Fire, which joined the league for its second season in 1997, and the Houston Dynamo, which was founded in 2005. In 2002, they joined Silicon Valley Sports in their ownership of the San Jose Earthquakes before buying the remainder of the club in 2003. Their final acquisition was the MetroStars in 2001 before selling them to another big corporation that has established significant soccer ownership interests around the world, Red Bull in 2006.[93]

---

91 Ibid.

92 Ibid.

93 Ibid.

The lack of diversity within the ownership pool led to a conflict of interest because many investor-operators during the formative years of the league owned multiple clubs, thus their concerns ran deeper than the performance of a single team on the pitch, especially when both teams on the pitch were owned by the same person or group. The steady investor-operators did, however, ensure the longevity of the league, as they were deeply invested in its success due to the founders' unique business model.

In the first season of MLS in 1996, the league, consisting of ten teams, was divided into two regional conferences. The East and the West. All ten of the teams received four players from the league to begin to fill their squad. Two of the players were foreign while two were from the United States. These players were known as "marquee players" and were signed to the league beginning in January 1995 and continued until the kickoff of the league in April 1996. The league also held numerous drafts to help the teams fulfill their obligation of at least eighteen players in squads.[94]

They had an open tryout in which they invited hundreds of people to try out. Following the tryouts, teams had their chance to draft individuals who had tried out.[95] They also held a draft of college soccer players that resembled the draft that was popular within the NBA, NFL, MLB, and NHL.[96]

---

94 FRASER v. MAJOR LEAGUE SOCCER, 284 F.3d 47, (1st Cir. 2002).

95 Dave McKibben, "Pro Soccer Combine Begins Today at UC Irvine," *Los Angeles Times*, January 6, 1996.

96 "1996 MLS College Draft," MLS, March 4, 1996.

Even after all of these tryouts and drafts and marquee players, teams had holes to fill within their squad, so the league opted to allow teams to participate in the more common worldwide transfer market in all of world football.[97] This meant teams could purchase the rights of world players to complete their squads from other teams around the world, especially South America and Europe.

To promote the development of the sport locally rather than just promote the buying and selling of established world superstars, MLS established a pipeline between the existing lower-tier American clubs and American college stars through a series of drafts.[98] They also implemented an American rule known as a salary cap that was also commonplace within other American sports leagues such as the NFL, NBA, and NHL. No player was allowed to receive more than $192,500.[99] These rules made it very difficult to recruit established players from established leagues who would not have been enthusiastic at the idea of taking a pay cut to join an unestablished, upstart league.

They needed a salary cap once again due to the failure of the NASL. Because many teams were forced into paying an arm and a leg to stay competitive by importing foreign players, they decided to cap salaries so that if foreign players came, they couldn't force the teams into absurd deals.

---

97 FRASER v. MAJOR LEAGUE SOCCER.

98 "Then and Now: An examination of key differences in MLS from 1996 to now," San Jose Earthquakes, accessed Jul 7, 2020.

99 "Then and Now: How MLS Has Changed Since 1996," San Jose Earthquakes, March 30, 2016.

The measures they enacted to encourage American soccer was also based on the shortcomings of the NASL. To follow the vision of the founders who did so to appease FIFA by promoting the sport domestically, they needed to continue the domestic growth of the club. Domestic growth is intertwined with the development of local players and heroes. In addition to their mission, growing the sport in the United States had huge financial benefits for the league as well because it effectively grew their fan base and number of customers.

***

Measures like those of MLS are not unheard of though. In 2010, the FA established a rule for the Premier League. Teams could have first-team squads of up to twenty-five players, the only caveat being that they had to have at least eight homegrown players in the squad. The rule became known as the "Homegrown Player Rule."[100]

A homegrown player was defined as anyone who had spent three or more years in England before the age of twenty-one. While almost all players who fulfilled that criteria were Englishmen, the rule did not limit the nationality of the players.[101]

Arsenal's Cesc Fabregas is the best example of a player who fulfilled the criteria; having joined Arsenal at sixteen, he was a Spanish international throughout his entire career. Also, clubs did not need eight homegrown players; they merely

100 "Premier League Home Grown Players rule: How does it work?" *Goal*, March 9, 2018.

101 Ibid.

could not have more than seventeen foreign players, which left eight open spots, which would then have to be home-grown talents.[102]

The point of the rule was to promote the development of English youth and give Premier League teams an incentive to invest in their youth systems. The plan has evidently been working. A glance at the England squad sheet and their stunning performance at the 2018 World Cup would indicate that over the last ten years, the quality of the English team has improved dramatically.[103]

***

In more attempts to Americanize the sport, MLS integrated other rules that were much more familiar to the American fan base and were intended to make the game more popular among American supporters. They decided to change the timing system. Instead of the traditional ways of most of world football, in which they counted up to ninety minutes and had stoppage time to make up for injuries and stoppages within the game, MLS decided to make the timing system count down from ninety to a dedicated ending buzzer at zero, rather than begin at zero.[104]

This was similar to the style of timing used by other American sports. Basketball and football leagues' fans were used to watching games with many stoppages and slowly grinding

---

102 Ibid.

103 Ibid.

104 "Then and Now: An examination of key differences in MLS from 1996 to now," San Jose Earthquakes.

through the games, which always counted down. MLS also decided to implement a new rule in which they would not finish games as draws. They did this because they did not want to dissuade fans from enjoying the sport by trying to eliminate the tedium of a draw.[105]

To add excitement to the games, MLS added a rule which made all games that finished as a draw after full-time proceed to penalty kicks. MLS officials believed this would greatly excite many American fans and lead to a much more interesting finish to games. The new system led to a different method of scoring games as well in terms of points for the league tables.

Normally, teams receive three points for wins as was traditional in England and the rest of world football, but in the absence of draws, which had been eliminated—with penalty shootouts in their place—they decided to award points differently to teams that achieved traditional wins vs. teams that had achieved penalty shootout wins. Teams that won the penalty shootout got one point, whereas the losers of traditionally finished games and penalty shootouts received zero points in both situations.[106]

***

The attempts of the league to promote American soccer over foreign, primarily South American and European soccer, has been successful. Many players who received player of the

105 Ibid.

106 Ibid.

week awards and player of the month awards and other honors for their performances in the league were representing the United States in the World Cup.

Seventeen out of the twenty-four players who were awarded a player of the week honor throughout the first season were American players (Eric Wynalda, Brian McBride twice, Marcelo Balboa, Bo Oshoniyi, Preki, John Doyle, Mark Dodd, Mark Chung, Tony Meola twice, Paul Bravo, Cobi Jones, Joe-Max Moore, Brad Friedel twice, and Brian Maisonneuve) while the remainder were from other South American and North American countries. The Scoring Champion (Roy Lassiter), Goalkeeper of the Year (Mark Dodd), and Defender of the Year (John Doyle) awards also went to Americans along with the Goal of the Year (Eric Wynalda) and the Rookie of the Year (Steve Ralston). The MVP award, however, went to Carlos Valderamma, a Colombian player famous for his tremendous hair. The Coach of the Year award was also granted to a foreigner, Thomas Rongen, a coach from The Netherlands.[107]

Six of the ten top scorers, including Roy Lassiter, who dominated the league scoring twenty-seven goals in a thirty-two-game season, were American. Lassiter scored thirty-seven goals in total for Tampa Bay in sixty appearances for the club. In addition, eleven of the total thirteen goalkeepers who clocked more than one thousand minutes between the sticks during the season were also American.[108]

---

107 "Major League Soccer: 1996," SoccerStats.us, accessed July 7, 2020.
108 Ibid.

- The Player of the Week award is given to the player that performs the best across the league each week.
- The Scoring Champion award, also known as the golden boot, is given to the player who scores the most goals throughout the season.
- The Goalkeeper of the Year award is given to the goalkeeper who has kept the cleanest sheets throughout the season.
- The Defender of the Year award is given to the player who plays in a defensive spot, usually a fullback or center back and exemplifies the highest level of defending prowess throughout the season.
- The Goal of the Year award is an award given to the player who managed to net the most impressive goal that season.
- The Rookie of the Year award is given to the best player who has no prior professional experience.
- The MVP, or Most Valuable Player, award is intended for the player who was most irreplaceable, important, and changed the league the most throughout the season. The reward is typically reserved for the player who performs at the highest level each season, although it's generally awarded to a midfielder or forward.
- The Coach of the Year award is given to the coach who did the best job leading their team throughout the season.
- Awards, including Player of the Week, Goalkeeper of the Year, Defender of the Year, Rookie of the Year, MVP, and Coach of the Year, that cannot be determined objectively are put to the vote by MLS players, staff, executives, and media.[109]

---

109 Alicia Rodriguez, "Carlos Vela is 2019 Landon Donovan MLS Most Valuable Player," *MLS*, November 4, 2019.

***

All in all, the first season was a success for Americans within the sport, and it was a success for the league. The first season drew an average of more than seventeen thousand fans to each game, which is almost three thousand more fans per game than the NASL had drawn even at the height of the league in the late seventies.[110] Despite competitiveness issues, MLS had done a successful job of building a league that got off the ground well and was already greatly appreciated by fans. The league, however, still needed some improvement, as there were still only ten teams and a very sloppy playoff system that excluded only two teams from the chance of playing in the league finals.

Tampa Bay won the first season on the league table, but in the final playoffs after the regular season, D.C. United, who had finished third in league play triumphed over LA Galaxy, the winners of the Western Conference, and racked up the second-most points in the league table during the season.[111]

The following season, however, the league had greatly diversified when compared with the American-dominated first season. The plurality of the award winners had still been American, but many more non-American players and nations were represented than the previous season. They had won twelve of the twenty-four players of the week awards while

---

110 "USA: Major League Soccer 1996: Attendance: Home matches," worldfootball.net, accessed July 7, 2020; "NASL 1968-84: A review of the Golden Era," NASL, accessed July 7, 2020.

111 "Standings," MLS, updated July 7, 2020; "HIGHLIGHTS: LA Galaxy vs. D.C. United | MLS Cup 1996," MLS, October 20, 1996.

players of only three nationalities had secured the title more than once that season with the likes of Carlos Vaderamma and Anthony de Avila from Colombia; Guiseppe Galderisi and Roberto Dondani from Italy; and the two-time winner Gilmar from Brazil all receiving the weekly award.[112]

Once again, the United States fielded the vast majority of the goalkeepers during the season, with nine out of the eleven who had tallied more than one thousand minutes on the pitch being American players. But the field in which the Americans really outshone the other contenders within the league was the end-of-season awards. The Most Valuable Player award (Preki), the Scoring Champion award (Preki), The Defender of the Year award (Eddie Pope), the Goalkeeper of the Year award (Brad Friedel), The Rookie of the Year award (Mike Duhany), the Coach of the Year award (Bruce Arena), and the Fair Play Award (Mark Chung) were all received by Americans. In fact, the only award received by a non-American was the Goal of the Year award, which went to Bolivian Marco Etcheverry.[113]

KEY TAKEAWAYS:

- At the start, MLS made a conscious effort to avoid the pitfalls faced by the NASL.
- Initially, the league largely promoted the game domestically, growing American soccer talent significantly.

112 "Major League Soccer: 1997," SoccerStats.us, accessed July 7, 2020.

113 Ibid.

CHAPTER 8

EARLY MLS EXPANSION

In the 1998 season, the league experienced its first of many expansions. The Chicago Fire and Miami Fusion both joined the league, propelling it to a total of twelve teams instead of ten.[114] At the conclusion of the season, the Americans maintained their status as league leaders, as most of the players who succeeded on the pitch and within the record books were Americans.[115]

One astonishing event from this season was when the Chicago Fire, the newly created franchise, pulled off the winning of the MLS Cup. They won the final championship trophy of the league, for which all twelve teams were competing, in their inaugural season.[116] Their victory showed that the league was wide open to any team that intended to prioritize winning the league.

114 "Standings: 1998," MLS, updated July 8, 2020.

115 "Major League Soccer: 1998," SoccerStats.us, accessed July 8, 2020.

116 Dylan Butler, "MLS Classics: Chicago Fire make history in 1998 MLS Cup vs. DC United," *MLS*, May 24, 2020.

The following year, the United States Women's National Team won their second FIFA Women's World Cup in ten years.[117] Not only did they win the highest level of women's soccer, but they did it on home soil, with one of the most inspiring generations of athletes leading the team to success. That generation inspired the little girls who grew into what is now a National Team that has won the last two World Cups.

By 2002, however, the league had returned to ten teams, as the two Florida clubs had folded in February before the start of the season. Miami Fusion had decided to end their operations and participation within MLS because they were not successful, and they subsequently received very little local interest.[118] The Tampa Bay Mutiny, one of the ten founding clubs, dissolved because the team also sparked little local interest.[119]

Despite MLS's struggles, the U.S. Men's National Team performed well in 2002. Led by MLS players, such as Clint Mathis and young stars such as Landon Donovan, the team made a surprise run to the quarterfinals, reigniting soccer excitement in the U.S.[120] MLS was the primary beneficiary—adding two teams in the 2005 season and increasing local attendance and community support across the league.

---

117 "World Cup Women: 1999," SCOREBOARD, accessed July 8, 2020.

118 Chris Smith, "MLS failed in Miami before. Will David Beckham's team be any different?" *The Guardian*, January 30, 2018.

119 Eugene Rupinski, "The Forgotten Story of the Tampa Bay Mutiny," *Brotherly Game*, February 5, 2014.

120 Clemente Lisi, "Remembering the USMNT in the 2002 World Cup," *US Soccer Players*, October 14, 2013.

From 2001 to 2002, league attendance went up just over 11 percent.[121]

They gained two more teams in the West instead of in Florida. Real Salt Lake, based in Salt Lake City, and Chivas USA played their inaugural seasons in 2005.[122] Dave Checketts, who had some experience in sports ownership with the Utah Jazz and was the president of the New York Knicks in the 1990s, was the primary investor-operator of Real Salt Lake.[123] Chivas USA, on the other hand, has a much more interesting origin story than the founding of Real Salt Lake.

They were an extension of the Mexican side, Guadalajara, commonly referred to as just Chivas, in the United States. Chivas USA was based in Carson, California, which is just outside of Los Angeles, California.[124] Los Angeles already had a very successful team though. The Los Angeles Galaxy had drawn the most support over the first ten years—averaging the highest attendance of any club in 2004 by more than six thousand fans per game.[125] This did not bode well for the young Chivas subsidiary.

***

121 "2001 Major League Soccer Stats," FBREF, accessed July 8, 2020; "2002 Major League Soccer Stats," FBREF, accessed July 8, 2020.

122 "Standings: 2005," MLS, updated July 8, 2020.

123 Morgan Jones, "Dave Checketts' son posts video of parents opening assignment to serve as mission president and companion," *DeseretNews*, December 29, 2017.

124 Clemente Lisi, "The short history of Chivas USA," *US Soccer Players*, May 4, 2020.

125 "2004 Major League Soccer Stats," FBREF, accessed July 8, 2020.

Guadalajara began Chivas USA to capitalize on the cultural influences that Latino communities have had in American Soccer.

As Grant Wahl, an acclaimed journalist who has covered soccer professionally for over twenty years, said in his podcast when explaining the new name *Fútbol with Grant Wahl,* "American Soccer has had a lot of cultural influences, obviously, and one of the biggest ones is the Latino community. My soccer roots come in part from living in Argentina, and I've spent plenty of time over the years in Mexico and other Spanish-speaking soccer capitals, which include lots of cities in the United States."[126]

Wahl's analysis can be backed up with numbers as well.

A May 2020 survey by Statista found that 28 percent of Hispanic respondents were either avid or casual MLS fans, while only 19 percent of African American respondents and 18 percent of white respondents were avid or casual MLS fans. They did, however, find that 27 percent of respondents who identified in some way not mentioned previously were avid or casual MLS fans, and 20 percent, two points higher than the 18 percent of avid Hispanic fans, of the "other" respondents were avid MLS fans.[127]

---

126 Grant Wahl, "Welcome to Fútbol with Grant Wahl," May 12, 2020, in *Fútbol with Grant Wahl*, produced by Grant Wahl, podcast, MP3 audio, 1:23.

127 Christina Gough, Level of interest in Major League Soccer in the United States as of May 2020, by ethnicity, distributed by Statista.

Not only are the fans overwhelmingly Hispanic, but the league itself proportionally employs more Hispanic athletes than other big American Sports Leagues. In 2017, MLS had 111 players from Latin America, with 316 players from the United States and Canada.[128] That's more than one player from Latin America for every three American or Canadian players. In 2019, MLB had 323 players from Latin America to the 1027 American and Canadian Players.[129] The NFL has 3 players out of a total pool of 1649 players of almost all Americans or Canadians from Latin America.[130] The NBA, from a total number of 450 players, has only 6 Latin American Players.[131] The NHL does not have a single player from Latin America.[132]

While many of these sports are way behind MLS in terms of league diversity, MLB and MLS are close in terms of Latin America to Northern America ratio. Where MLS really proves the point, however, is in the demographics of MLB fandom.

A Vox survey from 2017 found that only 9 percent of MLB fans identify as Hispanic, while 83 percent identify as white and 9 percent identify as African American.[133] The U.S. Cen-

128 "MLS once again the most diverse league in North America," MLS, accessed July 8, 2020.

129 "Major League Baseball Players by Birthplace During the 2019 Season," Baseball Almanac. accessed July 8, 2020.

130 "Player Birthplaces," Pro Football Reference, accessed July 8, 2020.

131 "NBA rosters feature 108 international players in 2019-20: Players active for opening-night rosters come from 38 countries and territories," NBA, October 22, 2019.

132 "Active NHL Players Totals by Nationality: Career Stats," QuantHockey, accessed July 8, 2020.

133 Alvin Chang, "This is why baseball is so white," *Vox*, updated October 24, 2017.

sus Bureau reported in 2019 that 18.5 percent of Americans identified as "Hispanic or Latino."[134] While more Major League Baseball players came from Latin America than Major League Soccer players, MLS has almost double the support from the Hispanic community. Moreover, while MLS fans are disproportionately Hispanic compared to national demographics, MLB fans are disproportionately non-Hispanic.

Much of the data referencing countries of origin should, however, be taken with a grain of salt because many American born players of not only soccer but also baseball, and every other sport identify themselves as Hispanic. Having been born in a Latin American country does not predetermine the exact number of players of Hispanic ethnicity.

The data does, however, point to two clear trends in America. Many MLS players are Latin American, and many MLS fans are Hispanic. Guadalajara, a Mexican club, used these trends to try to capitalize on the millions of Hispanic people living in Los Angeles, where, in 2019, 48.6 percent of Angelenos identified as "Hispanic or Latino."[135]

***

The two fledgling teams, Chivas USA and Real Salt Lake, proved their inexperience, finishing bottom of the West and eleventh and twelfth overall. Real Salt Lake, finishing

---

134 U.S. Census Bureau, "All Topics, Los Angeles, California, United States," QuickFacts: Los Angeles city, California; United States, accessed July 8, 2020.

135 Ibid.

eleventh, racked up a mere twenty points from thirty-two games—winning only five, drawing five, and losing twenty-two games (by this point, the league had decided to revert to traditional point allocation rules. Draws were finished as draws, and each team was awarded one point for their participation in the draw instead of the previous rules in which games that finished level went into penalty shootouts). Chivas finished with even fewer points, winning only four games, drawing six, and losing twenty-two games. They amassed only eighteen points. Both teams finished well below the veteran tenth place team, Columbus Crew, which only missed out on the playoffs by seven points and finished eighteen points higher than Real Salt Lake and more than double the points of Chivas.[136]

In 2006, the league was altered again. The Austrian company Red Bull bought New York/New Jersey MetroStars. Yes, the energy drink company bought a soccer team in New York City.[137] Surprisingly, the energy drink tycoon seemed to be extremely interested in the football club industry.

Perhaps they were attempting to take over the sport through multiple teams spread across the world. Red Bull has already bought up a team that now competes within the German first division, the Bundesliga, in the form of Red Bull Leipzig, which they acquired while they were in the German fifth division in the 2009–10 season.[138] They also acquired the

136 "Standings: 2005."

137 Jack Bell, "Red Bull Buys the MetroStars," *The New York Times*, March 9, 2006.

138 Alex Bysouth, "RB Leipzig: How did Red Bull build a Champions League side from scratch?" *BBC*, February 20, 2020.

Austrian Club SV Austria Salzburg shortly before buying out MetroStars in 2005 and renamed it Red Bull Salzburg.[139] Red Bull Salzburg now dominates the Austrian first division year after year, qualifying for the UEFA Champions League regularly and having success within the group stage round regularly as well.

The continuing diversity of ownership in the league was a good sign. The steady net increase of teams was also a good sign, but perhaps the most promising sign was consistency. Despite additions of teams, from 1998 to 2006, the league's attendance data stayed almost eerily similar, except for the jump in 2002 due to the excitement generated by the World Cup. In 1998 on average, 73 percent of capacity was met.[140] In 2006, 72 percent.[141] In 1998, the average attendance at a game was 15,114.[142] In 2006, it was 15,113.[143]

While stagnation could be a bad sign, the consistency of MLS proved they were not doomed for the failure faced by the American Soccer League and the North American Soccer League.

---

139 "Club History," FC Red Bull Salzburg, accessed July 8, 2020.

140 Russell Scibetti, "Looking at MLS Attendance Over the Years," *KORE Software* (blog), March 26, 2019.

141 Ibid.

142 Ibid.

143 Ibid.

KEY TAKEAWAYS:

- MLS began to grow with the addition of more teams.
- Latin America had a huge cultural impact on soccer in the United States.
- Around the turn of the century, the U.S. was doing well on the international stage.
- MLS was beginning to stagnate.

CHAPTER 9

RELOCATION AND GEOGRAPHY

The other big shift within the league that occurred during the 2006 season was the movement and relocation of the recently renamed San Jose Earthquakes to Houston, Texas. The club, experiencing trouble with their investor-operator, Anschutz Entertainment Group, which couldn't secure them a stable soccer stadium to play in, had decided to move to Houston and rebrand as well, becoming the Houston Dynamo.[144]

The shift was the first example of a club within MLS switching cities. This sort of movement had been extremely common within the NASL, which was one reason MLS was determined to provide locked-in investor-operators who were dedicated to their clubs and had paid hefty fees to enter their clubs into the league. One reason was that these

144 "Briefs and other stuff: Earthquakes of MLS moving to Houston," *Daily Press*, December 16, 2005.

investor-operators would have stronger community ties, so fewer franchise relocations would result.

The movement of a club from one city to another, although not popular, is commonplace in American sports. Many teams across all leagues have been forced to relocate due to financial problems, lack of support, or just the preference of the owner. In the last ten years, plenty of NFL teams have relocated. The Saint Louis Rams became the Los Angeles Rams (again) in 2016.[145] The San Diego Chargers became the Los Angeles Chargers (also again) in 2017 after having left the city for San Diego in the sixties.[146] The consistently nomadic Oakland Raiders are set to move to Las Vegas before the start of the 2020 season.[147] Perhaps the most famous example, however, was when the Cleveland Browns announced a movement to Baltimore "overnight" in 1995.[148] Movement has sparked outrage across all these clubs' fans.

Relocation is not limited to the NFL though. There are examples of teams relocating in other American sports leagues as well. Within the NHL, the Atlanta Thrashers moved to Winnipeg in 2011, becoming the Winnipeg Jets, the name of a previous NHL club that had relocated to Phoenix.[149] Within

---

145 Jack Dickey, "Lessons from the St. Louis' Rams Move to Los Angeles," *Time*, January 28, 2016.

146 David Garrick, "Chargers announce move to Los Angeles," *The San Diego Union-Tribune*, January 12, 2017.

147 Paul Gutierrez, "Raiders move to Las Vegas approved 31-1," *ESPN*, March 27, 2017.

148 Rich Exner, "How the story of the Cleveland Browns moving to Baltimore unfolded – November 1995," *cleveland.com*, updated May 19, 2019.

149 Rod Nickel, "Atlanta Thrashers moving to Winnipeg," *Fox News*, updated November 20, 2014.

the MLB during the fifties and sixties, the Northeast, densely populated with professional baseball teams, experienced a mass exodus as teams expanded to Western cities.

The Boston Braves moved to Milwaukee; the Philadelphia Athletics moved to Kansas City and then to Oakland later in the sixties; the Brooklyn Dodgers moved to Los Angeles; the New York Giants moved to San Francisco; and the Washington Senators moved to Minneapolis, Minnesota.[150] Their successor, also called the Washington Senators, decided to relocate to Dallas and become the Texas Rangers.[151] Within the NBA, the Charlotte Hornets moved to New Orleans, Louisiana, and became the Pelicans a few years later.[152] In 2008, the Seattle SuperSonics moved to Oklahoma City, becoming the Thunder.[153]

***

This concept is all but unheard of within the United Kingdom and the realm of British soccer. In 2003, however, Milton Keynes Dons, previously known as Wimbledon

---

150 Craig Calcaterra, "Today in baseball history: Braves announce moves from Boston to Milwaukee – Hardball Talk," *NBC Sports*, March 13, 2020; Max Rieper, "Losing a sports team: The relocation of the Kansas City Athletics," *Royals Review*, January 20, 2016; Scooby Axson, "When did the Dodgers move to LA? Los Angeles relocation date," *Sports Illustrated*, September 12, 2017; Dana Mozley, "The Giants baseball team announces move to San Francisco in 1957," *New York Daily News*, August 18, 2015; Jacob Bogage, "Washington baseball history: A beginner's guide to the Senators, Grays, and Nationals," *The Washington Post*, October 22, 2019.

151 Bogage, "Washington baseball history."

152 Elliott Teaford, "Hornets on Way to New Orleans," *Los Angeles Times*, May 11, 2002.

153 Jim Brunner and Sharon Pian Chan, "Sonics moving to Oklahoma City," *The Seattle Times*, updated February 17, 2012.

FC, uprooted and left Wimbledon for Milton Keynes.[154] This relocation is the only example of a movement like this in English soccer, and it was clear they were following the American strategy of movement, but this was a highly unsuccessful plan.

Almost immediately after the relocation plan was announced, the Wimbledon faithful decided to change allegiance and realigned as Wimbledon Faithful. Confusing? It is. Once Wimbledon FC announced their plans to relocate to Milton Keynes, the Wimbledonians decided to back their new club AFC Wimbledon. The club was founded in 2002 after the FA approved the movement of Wimbledon FC to Milton Keynes. There, they eventually became MK Dons to avoid confusion and to distance themselves from their Wimbledonian past.[155]

The remaining AFC Wimbledon had a meteoric rise, while the ex-Wimbledon FC's success faltered. MK Dons fell to the depths of League 2 before joining their rivals AFC Wimbledon in League 1, where both teams were competing for promotion to the Championship in the 2019–20 season.[156]

The lack of club relocation in England can be tied to one essential reason. Fandom is based much more upon geography in England than within the United States. There are over ninety professional football teams within the football

---

154 "Wimbledon become MK Dons FC," *The Guardian*. June 21, 2004.

155 Ibid.

156 "Our history," AFC Wimbledon, accessed July 8, 2020.

league for the English to choose from. Most fans choose to support a local club regardless of level.

While it's true that many people from England—and the rest of the world in this age of intense globalization—support a team based upon the team's success, there are some stigmas against that. In England, it is looked down upon for a fan new to the football league to jump onto the bandwagon of one of the large, successful clubs. In England, six large clubs have significantly more payroll and, thus, they almost exclusively compete for cups and titles. These six clubs are Liverpool, Manchester United, Manchester City, Chelsea, Tottenham Hotspur, and Arsenal. They have won twenty-five of the twenty-seven Premier League titles, twenty-four of the twenty-seven FA Cups, and nineteen of the twenty-seven League Cups since the beginning of the Premier League Era until the 2018–19 season.[157]

Most English Football fans opt to support their local team instead because they are connected to their local team through proximity, a sense of belonging with the rest of the fans, and a sense of loyalty against local rivals who tend to share the virtue of proximity.

***

In America, it's not uncommon to find fans of teams across the country. While it's true that many fans support their

157 "English Football final tables pages," English Football League Tables, accessed July 8, 2020; "FA Cup Seasons," English Football League Tables, accessed July 8, 2020; "League Cup Seasons," English Football league Tables, accessed July 8, 2020.

local team, whether it be Bostonians supporting the Red Sox or Kansas Citians supporting the Royals, it's much more common for most, if not all, teams to have a national following among Americans. This is because most Americans have no sense of connection to anyone's team because, in most cases, the team does not reside right up the road or down the street. Thus, this is not a "hometown" team but a nearby team. U.S. sports leagues have attempted to create associations through television and radio rights deals, allowing relative geographic concentration. But with the internet and the advent of regional sports television channels, a fan of the Kansas City Royals can watch every game from virtually everywhere in the world, not just Kansas City.

For a resident of Omaha, Nebraska (such as the author), a Metropolitan area of almost one million people, the pickings for professional sports teams are slim. The nearest Major League Baseball teams are the Kansas City Royals, which is about three hours or 185 miles away; the Chicago Cubs and White Sox, which is about seven hours or 468 miles away; the Minnesota Twins, which is about 5.5 hours or 377 miles away; and the St. Louis Cardinals, which is about 6.5 hours or 433 miles away.[158] These teams (and every other team in the country, especially the successful ones) all draw support from the roughly one million people

158 "Directions for Driving from Omaha, Nebraska to Kansas City, Missouri," Google Maps, accessed July 8, 2020; "Directions for Driving from Omaha, Nebraska to Chicago, Illinois," Google Maps, accessed July 8, 2020; "Directions for Driving from Omaha, Nebraska to Minneapolis, Minnesota," Google Maps, accessed July 8, 2020; "Directions for Driving from Omaha, Nebraska to St. Louis, Missouri," Google Maps, accessed July 8, 2020.

in Omaha, but it's also not uncommon to see fans of the remaining twenty-five Major League Baseball teams within the city. Omahans have no geographic sense of connectedness to their teams. This may be the case for many people around the U.S., which leads to the diversity of fandom across the country.

Omaha to Kansas City, Chicago, Minneapolis, and St. Louis

Only about 129 million people are represented by professional baseball in their hometowns teams, which is less than 40 percent of the nation's population and leaves over two hundred million Americans without loyalty to a given team.[159] After all, the nearest team to Omaha by almost one hundred miles is the Kansas City Royals, a mere 185 miles, which is

159 U.S. Census Bureau, "Annual Estimates of the Resident Population: April 1, 2010 to July 1, 2019," Metropolitan and Micropolitan Statistical Areas Population Totals and Components of Change: 2010-2019, accessed July 8, 2020.

farther from Omaha than fourteen of the Premier League teams are from London.

Newcastle is 276 miles from the Center of London, only about ninety miles farther from London than the nearest MLB team to Omaha.[160] Manchester—the home of Manchester City and Manchester United—is around two hundred miles from London.[161] Liverpool—the home of Liverpool FC and Everton FC—is 213 miles from London.[162] And Burnley—the home of Burnley FC—is 237 miles from London.[163] This leaves fourteen of the twenty premier league teams closer to the largest population mass within the British Isles than any MLB, NBA, NFL, MLS, or NHL team is to the single city of Omaha, Nebraska within the United States. No wonder the fandom in England is much more tribal, while the fandom in the United States is more disinterested, distant, and disconnected from the heart of the sport for many Americans.

160 "Directions for Driving from Newcastle upon Tyne, United Kingdom to London, United Kingdom," Google Maps, accessed July 8, 2020.

161 "Directions for Driving from Manchester, United Kingdom to London, United Kingdom," Google Maps, accessed July 8, 2020.

162 "Directions for Driving from Liverpool, United Kingdom to London, United Kingdom," Google Maps, accessed July 8, 2020.

163 "Directions for Driving from Burnley, United Kingdom to London, United Kingdom," Google Maps, accessed July 8, 2020.

London to Newcastle-upon-Tyne, Liverpool, and Manchester

Not only do a minority of Americans not have a local team, but also many of those that do live in metro areas with professional sports teams are not locals. In 2017, 6.8 percent and 6.5 percent of those living in the Austin, Texas and Orlando, Florida metro areas, respectively had moved in from outside of the metro area within the last five years. More than one out every twenty people across both metros had moved there in the last five years.[164]

Some other big metros with Major League Soccer that share similar demographic trends include Seattle, Washington; Portland, Oregon; San Jose, California; Sacramento,

164 U.S. Census Bureau, "Metro Area-to-Metro Area Migration Flows," Metro Area-to-Metro Area Migration Flows: 2013-2017 American Community Survey, accessed July 8, 2020.

California; Salt Lake City, Utah; Denver, Colorado; and Nashville, Tennessee. Five percent to 6 percent of the population across these cities has moved there in the last five years.[165]

These trends coincide with general migration patterns within the United States. Many Americans are moving into the West and the South. All nine of the cities mentioned are either in the Southern or Western regions of the country.

These trends also paint a stark contrast with the opposite region. New York City, one of the most historic and clichéd examples of a place with a large migrant population, has the lowest of any team with Major League Soccer. In 2017, only 2.1 percent of New Yorkers had moved to New York from outside the metro area in the last five years. Obviously, New York is a massive metro area, and 2.1 percent of the population is still nearly half a million people, but the migration rates within different metros paint an easily distinguishable picture. Many American cities, especially those in the South and West, are not the city of birth for many of the residents.[166]

The fact that many Americans who live in the larger metro areas are not really "from" there provides evidence that they do not hold as deep a connection to the city as they would to a city where they have lived since their birth.

---

165 Ibid.

166 Ibid.

KEY TAKEAWAYS:

- Relocation is rampant within American Sports, but it has failed to take off in the United Kingdom.
- The United States is geographically challenged when it comes to building soccer culture.
- English Football League fandom is much more rooted in geographic and historic ties to teams than sports fandom in the United States.

CHAPTER 10

CONTINUED EXPANSION OF MLS IN THE UNITED STATES AND BEYOND

In 2007, Major League Soccer expanded yet again. Toronto FC, the first Canadian team to join MLS, was initiated for a franchise fee of just over $10 million.[167] The inclusion of Canadian athletic teams was not unusual for American sports leagues. Much like how many Welsh teams such as Cardiff City, Newport County, or Swansea City participate within the EFL system, many Canadian teams piggyback on the United States sporting systems, such as the Toronto Raptors in the NBA, the Toronto Blue Jays, and in the past, the Montreal Expos within the MLB.

The league where this is most prevalent, however, is the National Hockey League. Ice Hockey is the official National

167 "MLS approves Toronto expansion franchise," *CBC Sports*, updated November 12, 2005.

Winter Sport of Canada.[168] It's much more popular in Canada than the United States, where the answer to the question of which sport is most popular depends upon who you ask and where you are.

Seven out of thirty-one NHL teams participating in the 2019–20 season were Canadian.[169] At a glance, that may seem unequal, but if you compare the population, there is about a 1:10 ratio of Canadians to Americans and a 7:24 ratio of teams, which is about 1:3.[170] So, in theory, the Canadians have a higher representation in terms of teams. An NHL team exists for every five million Canadians compared to only one for every thirteen million Americans.[171]

Toronto FC became the first MLS team from Canada. They performed poorly in their first season in the East, much as Real Salt Lake and Chivas USA had done during their first seasons in the West. Toronto's team failed to generate many wins, but the team did lay a strong foundation for community support.[172]

2007 continued to be a year of weak performance by one of the recent expansion clubs. Real Salt Lake maintained their status at the bottom of the Western Conference. But

---

168 Ruaidhrí Carroll, "Ice Hockey: Canada's National Winter Sport," *Culture Trip*, March 29, 2017.

169 "Teams," NHL.com, accessed July 12, 2020.

170 "Canada Population (2020)," Worldometer, accessed July 12, 2020; "United States Population (2020)," Worldometer, accessed July 12, 2020.

171 Ibid.

172 "Standings," Toronto FC, accessed July 13, 2020; David Rudin, "Toronto FC brings soccer fans from across a diverse city together," *MLS*, December 10, 2016.

Chivas USA couldn't accumulate success and actually win the Western Conference that season, which was impressive given they had only recently joined the league and had opted to occupy Los Angeles, the same stomping ground of the already successful LA Galaxy.[173]

***

From 2008 to 2020, the league exploded. From thirteen clubs in 2007, MLS reached an astonishing twenty-six clubs by 2020, with the expectation of four more clubs by 2022. In 2008, the San Jose Earthquakes were finally reinstated after maintaining their rights to a club after their initial departure.[174] In 2009, Seattle Sounders FC, named after the past NASL Seattle Sounders, joined the league for $30 million.[175] In 2010, Philadelphia, the largest metropolitan statistical area without a franchise, bought its way in for the same $30-million franchise fee.[176] In 2011, Portland Timbers and the second Canadian football team, the Vancouver Whitecaps, entered the league for a franchise fee of $35 million each.[177] In 2012, Montreal Impact, the third and final (to this point) Canadian team, paid a franchise fee of around $40 million.[178]

---

173 "Standings," Toronto FC.

174 "History," San Jose Earthquakes, accessed July 13, 2020.

175 "It's official: Seattle to get MLS team in 2009," *The Seattle Times*, updated November 13, 2007.

176 Jonathan Tannenwald, "Kevin Durant becomes an owner of the Philadelphia Union to make an impact in Chester, not just in soccer," *The Philadelphia Inquirer*, updated June 15, 2020.

177 Ronald Blum, "Montreal to join MLS in 2012 as 19th team," *The Seattle Times*, updated May 7, 2010.

178 Ibid.

Despite the apparent popularity of owning a team, some signals of the overall structural weakness of the MLS system persisted. Even as owners were buying franchises for increasingly high franchise fees, not all the teams are financially viable. For example, Chivas, despite some on-the-field success, struggled financially. The parent team, Guadalajara, was experiencing increasing financial losses.[179]

The club was purchased in 2012 by a new owner that slashed employment and payroll to salvage financial viability. These efforts failed and led to the club's purchase by MLS. Strangely, just three days after the dissolution of the club, MLS accepted an offer granting an expansion team to Los Angeles of $110 million. Los Angeles FC was set to begin playing in the league in 2017.[180]

In 2015, New York City FC, the second New York club and the partner club of both Manchester City and the New York Yankees, paid an astounding $100-million-dollar franchise fee to enter the league.[181] The first Florida club since the failure of the market in the early 2000s, Orlando City, joined the same year, paying only $70 million, however.[182]

In 2017, Atlanta United joined for a franchise fee of $70 million, and Minnesota United followed suit the same year,

---

179 Clemente Lisi, "The short history of Chivas USA," *US Soccer Players*, May 4, 2020.

180 Ibid.

181 Jeff Z. Klein, "Whose side are you on?" *The New York Times*, February 27, 2015.

182 "Orlando awarded MLS expansion franchise," *USA Today*, November 19, 2013.

joining the league for a fee of $100 million.[183] In 2018, a year later than expected, Chivas USA's replacement, Los Angeles FC, joined the league, having paid $110 million for their franchise fee after buying the scraps of the old Los Angeles team from MLS.[184] In 2019, FC Cincinnati joined the league for a $150-million franchise fee.[185]

The 2020 MLS season kicked off in late February with Inter Miami CF and Nashville SC before being postponed until later in the summer. The Miami club, which was initiated for only $25 million by English football great David Beckham, was part of a special deal reached between Beckham and the league during his time with the LA Galaxy in 2007.[186] They agreed he would have the option to purchase an MLS club for $25 million if he so desired, and he used this option in 2014 to start Internacional Club de Futbol Miami, which is officially joining the league in the 2020 season.[187] Nashville SC, on the other hand, was required to pay the customary $150 million to join the league.[188]

MLS has announced additional expansion plans to be achieved by 2022. They intend to add four teams to reach the

---

183 Andy Greder, "Nothing 'United' about MLS expansion teams in Minnesota, Atlanta," *Pioneer Press*, March 10, 2017; Doug Roberson, "Atlanta get MLS franchise," *The Atlanta Journal-Constitution*, April 17, 2014.

184 Lisi, "The short history of Chivas USA."

185 Steve Watkins, "FC Cincinnati franchise value tops $400 million, Berding says (Video)," *Cincinnati Business Courier*, updated March 15, 2019.

186 Noah Davis, "Inter Miami's long wait for a home game made even longer by the coronavirus shutdown," *ESPN*, June 1, 2020.

187 Ibid.

188 Travis Yoesting, "Why MLS Expansion Fees Are so Damn High but Also Kind of a Great Deal," *The 18*, December 17, 2019.

high of thirty teams. MLS announced Austin's reception of a team in early 2019. They were required to pay the Cincinnati and Nashville expansion fee of $150 million.[189]

The new Sacramento team announced later that year, however, was expected to pay $200 million despite both teams joining in the same 2021 season. In August 2019, MLS announced the twenty-ninth expansion team, from Saint Louis. The new Saint Louis team is expected to join the 2022 season for the same $200-million fee as the Sacramento team.[190]

The most recent expansion to be announced was Charlotte, North Carolina, which was announced by MLS in October of 2019. They are expected to pay an unprecedented $325 million, a whopping 32.5 times the price paid by Toronto fourteen years earlier.[191]

- Toronto: $10,000,000
- San Jose: Renewed franchise after losing the initial club.
- Seattle: $30,000,000
- Philadelphia: $30,000,000
- Vancouver: $35,000,000
- Portland: $35,000,000
- Montreal: $40,000,000
- New York City: $100,000,000
- Orlando: $70,000,000
- Atlanta: $70,000,000
- Minnesota: $100,000,000

---

189 Ibid.

190 Ibid.

191 Ibid.

- Los Angeles: $110,000,000
- Cincinnati: $150,000,000
- Nashville: $150,000,000
- Miami: $25,000,000
- Austin: $150,000,000
- Sacramento: $200,000,000
- Saint Louis: $200,000,000
- Charlotte: $325,000,000

These franchise fees were the cost to purchase a club from the other owners and MLS itself. Unlike other parts of the world, the number of clubs in the U.S. with professional teams has been low due to cost, lack of community interest, poor access to players, and other cultural reasons. Thus, the U.S. did not and does not have an index of teams that could be asked to join MLS. Moreover, the MLS business model is dependent on franchise fees to enrich the other club owners. In other words, the environment in the U.S. is radically different from that of Europe.

***

Major League Soccer's expansion over the last decade has produced significant interest both nationally within the United States and internationally.

One apparent key change is that more players see MLS as a starting league. They can play well in the U.S. and then receive offers from teams in larger leagues with fewer payroll restrictions. For example, Miguel Almiron made his career at Atlanta United before securing a move to Premier League side Newcastle United in 2019.

All 30 Current and Planned MLS Teams

The rapid expansion has greatly increased both the value of the league and the value owners are willing to pay to purchase a club. Moreover, players see additional value as the scale of the MLS stage continues to rise and both the skill and reputation of the teams skyrocket. This has allowed players to find new homes and higher salaries.

Despite the rapid rise of MLS as a growing U.S. Domestic League, it's not compared regularly to the world's top leagues. The quality of the play still lags behind top international levels. And many of MLS's best players do not receive international acclaim when pitted against European club players at the World Cup. Thus, MLS still needs to improve in a variety of ways to be considered a top league—comparable in structure to the EPL or other top European leagues.

MLS's stature as a second-class league makes it somewhat unique in the U.S. landscape of domestic sports leagues. The NHL, NBA, MLB, and NFL are all considered the very top of their sport. Thus, top players come to the U.S. to play in those leagues—to reach their highest potential. Rarely do players dominate in the U.S. at the end of their careers after playing elsewhere. MLS, however, is rife with players playing out the end of their careers. So while MLS has achieved significant growth and financial success, just as Pelé came to the NASL at the end of his career, MLS still sees many top players only considering their clubs when they are in their thirties, near the end of their careers, such as Zlatan Ibrahimovic and Wayne Rooney.

***

MLS must proceed with caution. As they continue to add more and more expansion teams and continue to grow in support from American fans, they are approaching a fork in their path. One option is for them to continue their expansion as an American Sports League. MLS can solidify themselves as a league that books franchises, has a seasonal playoff, and recruits the most elite college athletes. That is the business model of an American sports league. Following this path would lead them into the same pitfalls that led to the demise of the NASL. Without plans beyond continued expansion, the league will expand beyond capacity and eventually fail.

The other option is for them to build upon the global success of the sport as a whole. The beautiful game is extremely popular and commonplace throughout the entire world, played on six continents and throughout over one hundred countries, vastly more popular and universal than any American sport. To do this, however, they would need to stray from the business model of an American sports league and take on that of a global soccer league.

MLS must make the conscious decision to opt for the success that many other soccer leagues around the world have achieved. It's not enough for them to build a national brand as other American sports have done. Instead, for MLS to be a top-tier international league, it must adopt a more international model—not that of the United States. While it's true that many American sports have uprooted and been ingrained in other cultures, such as baseball in Japan or basketball in Eastern Europe, none have done such a thing on anywhere near as large a scale as soccer has done throughout the world.

If they intend to succeed at the same level as other soccer leagues, they must recognize the global interest of the sport, and this means looking at the Premier League and other European leagues as their case studies rather than the NFL, NBA, MLB, and NHL. To mimic the European successes, they will have to focus on Europeanizing the league but maintain the addition of an American twist. Fundamentally, this book is about that twist.

If MLS chooses to attempt to build their success along the same lines as the NBA, NFL, MLB, and NHL, they will fail to reach the global recognition and excellence of many European leagues.

KEY TAKEAWAYS:

- Canadian and American sports are intertwined.
- MLS has engaged in rapid expansion since 2007.
- The league is nearing the end of expansion because they will either over-expand and fail or transition to a business model it can profit in a way that doesn't solely involve expanding the league.
- MLS needs to proactively strive to become a soccer league, not an American league.

PART 2

CHAPTER 11

MY INTRODUCTION TO THE BEAUTIFUL GAME

US Youth Soccer reports that the one hundred thousand kids who played soccer in 1974 have grown to over three million in 2018.[192] Youth Soccer in the U.S. has grown thirtyfold in the last forty-five years. I have the distinction of being one of those who joined the ranks of youth soccer since 1974.

I first became obsessed with playing the game through a close relationship with a babysitter—or au pair—from Germany who lived with my family for a year from 2013 to 2014. Her stay coincided with one of the biggest celebrations in the world's sport, the FIFA World Cup. Franzi is an avid football fan. She is a very loyal supporter of Borussia Dortmund, a consistent Champions League contender from the German Bundesliga. She is also an extremely dedicated fan of her national team, which happens to be one of the most formidable teams in world football.

192 "Who Is US Youth Soccer?" US Youth Soccer, accessed July 14, 2020.

That summer, we watched every single match we could stream. I will never forget the United States Men's National Team playing in their group stage matches as they beat Ghana on a late winner and drew Portugal, another world superpower, to make it into the next round despite a loss to Germany. I'll also never forget the heartbreak of losing to Belgium in extra-time.

After our elimination, I fell in love with the way the Germans could play what Pelé had referred to as "the Beautiful Game." Pelé, arguably the best player of all time, played during the fifties, sixties, and seventies. After concluding his professional career as a player, he released his autobiography titled *My Life and the Beautiful Game.* After his use of the phrase "the Beautiful Game," it became synonymous with the sport of football.

We watched the game mostly in our home (frequently in our "front room"). While U.S. National Team—both men's and women's—games were often available in group settings elsewhere, they were not in Omaha, where I spent most of my childhood.

The atmosphere in the front room as Germany decimated Brazil, the hosts, by an unprecedented six goals in the semifinal match was palpable. I remember Miroslav Klose's intense celebration as he became the nation's top goal scorer ever. As I fell in love with Germany, I fell in love with a specific player whose exquisite passes mesmerized me.

Mesut Ozil, who led the English Premier League in assists in the coming 2015–16 season and would eventually retire from international football at age thirty, was an inspiration. My eleven-year-old self watched on in awe over the next few years as I became fixated on Ozil and his club, Arsenal. I steadily fell in love with club football in addition to world football.

***

In the Summer of 2014, at the same time as the World Cup raged on in Brazil, in my home in Omaha, Nebraska, Franzi was preparing to leave, making way for Adriana. During the same World Cup experience, the two had conflicting views on who they wanted to win. After Spain's early exit, I figured Adriana would not really care how any team did because, either way, Spain no longer had any shot at winning the trophy. Boy was I wrong.

I first learned of Adriana's mysterious allegiances during the match between Switzerland and Argentina. I was hoping Switzerland would win because, generally, I tend to cheer for the underdog. I think this stems from my love of college basketball. After my bracket inevitably gets busted, I instantly maliciously hoped all higher seeds would win and everyone else's picks suffer just as much as mine. So naturally, I wanted Switzerland with their nameless faces to triumph over Argentina and the all-powerful Lionel Messi.

Assuming Adriana, having her team knocked out, would follow my college basketball logic, I called her down to the front room as the clock began to wind down on Messi and his white-and-blue-striped minions. As extra-time ebbed on, I began to relish the idea of another penalty shootout like the one I had witnessed between Brazil and Chile only days earlier. Then, in the 118th minute, just as penalties looked inevitable, Angel Di Maria, a player I later found out played for Real Madrid when he wasn't crushing the dreams of eleven-year-old children hoping to witness a penalty shoot-out on international duty, slotted a game-winner into the far corner from the right-hand side of the field, just past the outstretched arms of Swiss Keeper Diego Benaglio.

"GOOOOOOOOOAAAAAAALLL!" Adriana exclaimed jubilantly. How could she possibly want a decorated player like Messi to continue to thrive, I wondered rebelliously.

"I thought we wanted Switzerland to win?" I asked hesitantly, not wanting to upset the newcomer in my home.

"Well," she said, adopting the tone a teacher would use to explain that one and one made two, "Di Maria plays for Real Madrid, which means that we want him to score."

"I still don't really understand; I don't want Messi to win," I continued, slightly more confused than before.

"Real Madrid are the good guys," she explained impatiently, as if information like this was blatantly obvious from watching the game. "But Messi is not a good guy. He plays for the bad guys."

As I tried to wrap my head around good guys and bad representing the same nation and playing together, she continued showing me images of Barcelona and Real Madrid and explaining the basics of the rivalry—like how Real Madrid was sent by a deity in the hope of redeeming humanity and how Barcelona was probably founded by Satan himself. One time, she even tried to convince me that Gerard Pique was downright evil in the purest sense of the word, which I had some trouble believing.

"How can someone who plays for Spain be evil?" I would ask, knowing her justification would have something to do with his running around wearing red and blue on weekends.

As the au pairs came and went, I became infatuated with the commonality of the sport. Everybody played it, not just the United States and not just Britain. Around four billion people are involved with the sport in some capacity, whether it be through fandom or as a player. That is more than half of the world's population, which means enjoying soccer is potentially the most supported subjective stance presented anywhere. The endless possibilities provided by the worldliness of the game were enthralling.

***

Soccer is different from sports in the U.S. because there are numerous events. First, events such as the World Cup, Gold Cup, European Cup, or the Olympics are all played by the national team representing certain countries or areas. There are 211 countries that have men's national team representatives on the world's stage. This gets confusing because in 2020, Worldometer reported that there are 195 countries and 193 members of the United Nations.[193] Many of the additional

193 "How many countries are there in the world? (2020) – Total & List," Worldometer, accessed July 14, 2020.

sixteen countries stem from nations within other countries, such as the United Kingdom, where England, Wales, Scotland, and Northern Ireland all field their own squads rather than a United Kingdom National Team.

Historically, the U.S. Men's National Team has not performed well—missing the World Cup from 1950–1990. The U.S. Women's National Team, however, is the premier team in world football. The U.S. Women's National Team has appeared in every Women's World Cup, which was first played in 1991. Since their success in France in 2019, the team has won four of the eight total competitions, a track record significantly better than any other team in the world—men's or women's.

Beyond national teams, however, soccer players also play for clubs. Generally, the better the club, the more diversity within the club in terms of the players' nationality. For example, Arsenal had players from fourteen countries and three continents in the Spring of 2020.[194]

Arsenal, a club that has historically competed at a continental level within either the UEFA Champions League or the UEFA Europa League, also plays in the English domestic league—the English Premier League (EPL). They also compete in domestic tournaments, such as the Football Association Cup (FA Cup) and the League cup, currently known as the Carabao Cup. And as mentioned previously, they compete on a continental basis either within the UEFA Champions League or the slightly lesser-quality UEFA Europa League.

194 "Arsenal Squad: Men Information & Details," Arsenal.com, accessed July 14, 2020.

Both tournaments are played on the continental level, across Europe, with the best of Europe competing against each other for the final trophy.

***

The vastness of footballing competitions—from international football, to domestic football, to continental competitions—means that at some points during their careers, players are playing many games in a short amount of time. Using Mesut Ozil as an example, Arsenal played 112 games in the twenty-two-month period from August 2013 to May 2015.[195] Germany, Ozil's international side, played twenty-six games.[196] That's more than six games a month, or one to two games a week for almost two years. Ozil, of those 138 games, only played 87.

Most players peak around age twenty-six or twenty-seven. Ozil was no exception. He started the period at twenty-five and was twenty-six by May 2015. During the period, Arsenal and Ozil finished fourth and then third in the highly contested Premier League.[197] They also won the FA Cup twice, and the Community Shield—a preseason game between the previous season's FA Cup winners and Premier League champions—once. To cap it all off, Ozil won the World Cup

195 "Arsenal FC: Fixtures and Results 2013/2014," worldfootball.net, accessed July 14, 2020; "Arsenal FC: Fixtures and Results 2014/2015," worldfootball.net, accessed July 14, 2020.

196 "Germany National Team: Fixtures & Results 2013," worldfootball.net, accessed July 14, 2020; "Germany National Team: Fixtures & Results 2014," worldfootball.net, accessed July 14, 2020; "Germany National Team: Fixtures & Results 2015," worldfootball.net, accessed July 14, 2020.

197 "Honours," Arsenal.com, accessed July 14, 2020.

in the summer of 2014, with the German national side playing every game and collecting one goal and one assist across the seven games.

Ozil's grueling schedule in part explains why most players often peak around twenty-six or twenty-seven years old. The creative German playmaker, despite being a dominant force throughout his career, had his best seasons during the 2013–14 and 2014–15 campaigns featured above. The 2015–16 season was also particularly successful for the midfielder when he racked up the second-most assists ever recorded in a Premier League campaign by any player from any team with nineteen. During those seasons, he was twenty-five, twenty-six, and twenty-seven. Players peak so young because a single game, much less eighty-seven, is incredibly physically taxing. Each game is ninety minutes, and teams are only allowed three substitutions throughout the game. Eight or more of the eleven starters end up playing ninety minutes plus added time, with a single break at half time, while the three others tend to play between forty-five and ninety minutes depending on the coach and the game scenario. Additionally, a study done in 2013 by STATS reported that, on average, the ten field players (everyone except the goalkeeper) ran about seven miles per game, with the higher end being around nine-and-a-half miles, which doesn't even factor in training sessions required to stay in peak physical condition.[198] Older players are not physically equipped to endure as much rigor as a younger player.

198 Tracy Miller, "Which sports run the most? Stats from football, basketball, soccer and tennis show who burns the most shoe leather," *The New York Daily News*, April 4, 2013.

KEY TAKEAWAYS:

- My love for the game started with the induction of foreign cultures in my own house at the same time as the FIFA World Cup.
- The United States Men's National Team is not that good at soccer.
- The United States Women's National Team, on the other hand, is consistently dominant.

CHAPTER 12

CONTINUED LOVE FOR THE GAME

After my introduction into the game as a fan, the natural next step was for me to take that fandom to the next level, and to translate my love of the sport as a fan to a love for the sport as a player.

I began my ritual of watching football every Saturday morning as I folded laundry with my father, absorbing all his insights on the matches. He was a Tottenham Hotspur fan (In the soccer sphere, people refer to Tottenham Hotspur simply as "Spurs" or "the Spurs"), so naturally, a healthy rivalry began to develop, as Spurs and Arsenal are archrivals and located down the street from each other.

We would make bets for high stakes, such as five pushups, for North London Derby matches—in which Arsenal and Spurs, the two largest teams from North London would face off. We would poke fun at the other's poor performances against bottom-of-the-table Aston Villa, or money-laden

Manchester City. In other words, we developed a deep bond over football.

I had been playing the sport for my school's rec team since kindergarten and was always above average, but I was never that kid on the pitch who could turn people's legs to jelly with a series of quick stepovers (quick jabs over or around the ball used to confuse and trick the opposition on your intended direction). After falling in love with the sport though, I became obsessed with improving my own skill within the game. I spent hours kicking balls off the side of my house, trying to get as many juggles in a row as possible, and destroying my younger brother in one-on-ones.

Playing football and improving became a habit that furthered my enjoyment of the sport. None of my middle school classmates, in a class of sixty kids, shared my obsession. I played with some of them on the school team and they enjoyed scrimmaging at practice and playing games, but none of them could recite the names of the EPL's top goal scorers or list the promising young players who manned the Arsenal reserves. The void of fellowship with my peers prompted me to join a small club team.

After being cut from multiple tryouts. I landed at a local team that participated in the local youth league in the third or the fourth tier (my local league structure had a few separate divisions divided by skill, and my league was the third or fourth rung on the ladder with two or three better leagues available, in other words, not very good). After a couple of months of playing, a series of short-lived coaches, and a bit of a growth spurt, I emerged as one of our team's better defenders. I was finally surrounded by people who enjoyed the different aspects of the game, on varying levels granted, but they enjoyed it, nonetheless.

When a soccer fan says the word "tier" in the context of "second-tier French Football," they are referencing the position of their league in the various soccer pyramids. For the sake of this example, that would be the second-best league in France, which typically had opportunities for their teams to get promoted to the top league (first tier) and relegated to the league below (third tier). The phrase *tier* just describes the level at which a certain league participates. This can get very confusing the further down you get because as you go down, the number of leagues on each tier level increases to consolidate the leagues with less funding into geographic areas. Considering that my team was in the lower end of a local league youth setup, we were definitely not competing at a super high level.

One of my new teammates was a Tottenham Hotspur fan, and just like my dad and I, we established a friendly rivalry, but with a little more trash-talking. He facilitated my growth even further as a peer who not only enjoyed playing the game but enjoyed watching it just as much as I did. We began to watch football together and comment on various team performances and how different players had played in their most recent game. We loved to watch Filipe Coutinho in his Liverpool days, Harry Kane as he racked up goal after goal for the Spurs, and of course, my favorite, Mesut Ozil. This discussion not only helped me fall deeper in love with the sport, but it led to the development of heroes in my life with imagined personalities, and I could not help but yearn to see them in person.

***

For some context, my older brother, who had been a year ahead of me in school, had been promised a trip in eighth grade to China with my uncle. There was a catch though. The only condition was that he had to pay for 90 percent or more of the trip. After he succeeded in paying for his plane ticket and a week and a half in China, my parents struck a similar deal with me. I immediately set out to fund the trip that I imagined to the United Kingdom to see Arsenal play.

The summer before my eighth and final year at my K-8 Catholic school in Omaha, I set out on a mission to see Mesut Ozil and the rest of my heroic gunners in person. I undertook one of the most difficult and "Nebraskan" tasks I have ever striven to complete. I began detasseling corn to fund my mission.

For those not familiar with the concept, detasseling involves waking up at 4 a.m. every weekday and taking a bus to a cornfield to walk through and clean up after the automatic detasseling vehicle. This meant we walked through rows of corn plucking that golden tassel that sticks out of the top. However, most of the time, the tassel is often hard to find.

To avoid the heat of the afternoon sun, we began to trudge through the fields around 5 a.m. every morning. The average day entailed walking through massive cornrows, which act like ten-foot-tall blades of grass blanketed in glistening droplets of dew. The 5 a.m. strolls through dewy fields of corn were extremely tiring, wet, and cold. They were so cold because they were so wet, and they were so wet because to avoid corn rash—an extremely painful rash from being scratched by the stalks' serrated leaves—we were clothed head to toe, mainly in thick cotton.

Our outlandish uniform consisted of bright orange netted hats, not unlike those of beekeepers, worn-out t-shirts with socks pulled up to our shoulders and around our gloved hands, and to cap it off, we wore long socks and pants. These layers were extraordinarily good at not only collecting water but holding it for hours… for minimum enjoyment. Days like this were only a sliver of the torment I endured so that I might achieve my goal of traversing the United Kingdom in search of my heroes.

The following spring, after raising enough funds to pursue my dream, I joined Arsenal in London, the capital of the United Kingdom, where I stayed for about a week. The exposure to a culture much more influenced by football was jaw-dropping. I knew there were millions of football fans across the world but seeing so many concentrated in places such as Leicester Square or under the city in the London Underground or "tube" opened my mind to the reality. I knew I might never be able to experience this culture the same way ever again, so I lapped up every second of it and, with my dad's help, documented the entire trip with a series of photographs.

As I experienced London, I finally understood how so much could be in one place. The diversity and the density of the city were unparalleled by any other place I had been. The largest city I had visited before my journey to London had been Minneapolis, and the change of scenery astounded me. Petite wooded parks were tucked between urban blocks as if the urban habitat had just risen around the small emerald enclosures. Tiny Indian restaurants fit snugly between cafes and bookstores, serving curries the likes of which I had never known. This new culture was amazing. I fell in love with the city the same way I had fallen in love with the game that its citizens cultivated.

***

My next roadblock after overcoming the price of the endeavor was procuring tickets. In America, people don't care who you are when they sell you something; they just care about the weight of your wallet. In the United Kingdom, however, they might take a closer look at you and have one or two questions before selling you something like a ticket to an Arsenal game.

One reason is that scalping, the selling of tickets by informal third parties, is banned, and the ban is heavily enforced. This makes it impossible to show up to the stadium and just purchase tickets at random from a man holding them over his head. Another reason is that it's nearly impossible to buy them without a ticket-buying history. They do this to ensure the people who attend the games are true supporters, and it also makes it very difficult for people to infiltrate the opposing team's section of the stands. This was because in the 1970s and the 1980s, hooligans stationed in the opposing team's fan sections were disrupting games left, right, and center. This culture was richly explained in *Green Street* by the West Ham United Hooligans featured in the film.

Given the time we were there, we had one chance to watch Arsenal play an away game in Middlesbrough. Middlesbrough, on the edge of the Scottish Highlands, is about as far from London as you can get without entering Scotland—which has its own, separate league. The location of the game gave us three options: 1) buy tickets illegally and potentially face the consequences, 2) try to get tickets reserved for Middlesbrough fans who had a previous history with the club, or 3) convince Arsenal that despite our lack of history with the club, we were legitimate fans.

We opted for the option with the greatest chance of success (and a pretty low chance of us getting arrested): convince a relegation-bound club to sell two tickets to a couple of American tourists who wanted to watch their countryman Brad Guzan, the American international goalkeeper at the time.

It was so difficult to secure tickets to this game because Arsenal was a top-six side. This meant that Middlesbrough fans would turn up to watch because it's not very often that a team as good as a top-six side in the nation visits Middlesbrough to play their team—just about six times a year actually. After a few phone calls, the plan finally worked, and I found myself looking forward to residing within a crowd of Middlesbrough or "Boro" fans booing my beloved Arsenal.

My first hands-on experience with professional European football was incredible. Despite being surrounded by the enemy, I found myself enjoying every second of the game from my perch behind one of the goals. It was a Monday night in mid-April—the equivalent of Monday Night Football in the U.S. Despite it being spring, it was chilly (around 40° F) and there was some light rain.

I was enchanted by the unique chants that rang across the stadium (even though I could only understand about every third word). They liked one in particular that, as near as I could figure, entailed "going up a Boro." While I had no idea a "boro" was something one could go up, I assume it was a reference to their geographic location in the Northeast corner of England and described the trip Arsenal had made up to the Boro.

The first goal came off an Alexis Sanchez free-kick in the forty-second minute. The confused look and utter lack of movement from Brad Guzan on the complete other side of the pitch led me to believe that the wall of players lined up to block Sanchez's shot had gotten a touch on the ball, but unfortunately redirected it into their own net. In reality, Sanchez had just beat Guzan with a superb shot. There was so much dip on the ball that after clearing the wall by a couple of feet, the ball had lowered to almost ground level by the time it struck the back of the net. Guzan merely turned his head, completely stunned, as the lobbed ball sailed into the back of his net.

The lead was short-lived, however, lasting only a little longer than halftime. The reaction of the Middlesbrough faithful in the fiftieth minute after Alvaro Negredo's equalizer left me quivering. I heard the chant "BORO BORO BORO!" repeated loudly and clearly from every side.

During the second half, after the equalizer, while Guzan and his net were directly in front of the supporters of

Middlesbrough and me, I got to witness what I had been dreaming of since those 5 a.m. strolls through immense cornfields. In the seventy-first minute, Aaron Ramsey collected a cross down with his chest to the feet of my idol, Mesut Ozil. As he slotted the ball past Guzan, I had no choice but to cover my mouth to avoid revealing my utter glee to the thousands of now angry fans around me who had been hoping to secure at least one point (for a draw).

After my experience with football in the United Kingdom, it would have been impossible to forget how much I had enjoyed the experience and how much I now knew I loved the sport. This was my attitude as I began the next, and final, chapter of my football career.

***

Looking back, my initial experience with soccer draws many parallels with that of Nick Hornby and the childhood he documented in *Fever Pitch.* Hornby explained in detail how his father had introduced him to the game on his first trip to Highbury. I witnessed my first soccer match with my father.

"I fell in love with football as I was later to fall in love with women: suddenly, inexplicably, uncritically, giving no thought to the pain or disruption it would bring with it," he said, describing his conversion as a child. I too fell in love as a child, though I can't say I was quite as dedicated as he was.

Above all, though, Mr. Hornby and I both shared an immense love for Arsenal.

***

I started the year with the intent of running cross-country to condition for soccer in the spring. However, as I worked through the season with my brother, one of the faster varsity runners on the team, I realized I was actually half decent at running. By the end of the season, I was competing on the same level as the top seniors on the Junior Varsity (Second Team) Squad with me.

During the winter, I played indoor soccer with my classmates to prepare for the upcoming tryouts and spring season. While I was not the best-skilled player, I was tall, athletic, and had the endurance of a runner, which were good traits for a defender, my preferred position. I tried out in the spring, and after ultimately making the team, I started on my school's freshman team in the fullback position. As I worked my way through the season and competed on the highest level I had ever known, I began to realize just how difficult it was to compete at this level.

To continue preparing for my sophomore year of soccer, I worked out over the summer, doing dribbling, juggling, and touch drills in addition to the regimented running and lifting associated with cross-country. I knew I would have a challenge ahead of me—after all, my high school was extremely good, having won three state championships in the last decade and nine overall since 1987, when soccer became a high school sport in Nebraska.

The problem was that my "off season" for soccer was my "on season" for cross-country. The two sports both required me to practice after school. And my cross-country team was dominant that year, winning every meet we competed in, apart from the state championship meet, despite having beaten the eventual winners multiple times throughout the season. Four of the five seniors who had led the varsity team to victory ended up running in Division I the following year.

I had joined a club in the top tier of the age above mine over the summer to improve my skill and chances for making a better team that year, but the team, in addition to cross-country, school, and a social life, proved too much for me. I had to make one of the toughest decisions of my life.

I decided to quit football in the hope of running year-round with the track team in the spring. I promised myself I would maintain my connection with the sport though, if not by playing, then by expressing my fanaticism to my friends and by keeping up with the latest transfer news. This much more analytical position left me with some questions and some ideas about why the sport was the way it was in the United States.

***

The late introduction of the sport to the mainstream leaves a lot of room for growth in the United States. Whether Americans like it or not, football is the most-watched sport in the world, as well as the most played.[199] Consistent failure from

---

199 Sourav Das, "Top 10 Most Popular Sports in the World [Updated 2020]," *Sports Show*, June 4, 2020.

the country with the third-highest population in the world, as well as the richest in the world, is difficult to explain.[200]

Not all the United States is failing though. The Women's National Team, one of the sport's most dominant teams of all time, is possible in part by the promotion of women's soccer with Title IX and the success of women's soccer in the past. The United States is one of the most progressive countries in the world for women's rights. It makes sense that our women's soccer team would be formidable as well.

"Soccer really is only defined as a female sport in the United States. Everywhere else it is a male sport," said Eileen Narcotta-Welp, a soccer scholar at Wisconsin University-LaCrosse in an interview with *Business Insider* in 2019. "I wouldn't put it past them [United States Women's National Team] to continue to remain at the top of women's soccer for the foreseeable future," Narcotta-Welp continued when asked about whether the U.S. Women's National Team would continue to dominate.[201]

The sport does have a long way to go, especially for the men's team and players in the United States. For the United States to fully develop into the footballing powerhouse they could be, certain measures must be taken. Also, certain practices must be put to a stop immediately. For the United States to tap their potential, we must amend American Football.

---

200 "Population by Country (2020)," Worldometer, accessed July 14, 2020, "GDP by Country," Worldometer, accessed July 14, 2020.

201 David Anderson and Benji Jones, "US women's team moves on to the World Cup quarterfinal. Here's why American women are so good at soccer," *Business Insider*, June 25, 2019.

KEY TAKEAWAYS:

- I fell in love with the sport as a kid.
- I quit the sport long before my prime, like many other young people in America.
- American Football needs fixing.

CHAPTER 13

THE UNITED STATES VS. SOCCER

The five main sports in the United States are football, basketball, baseball, hockey, and soccer. All five have successful professional sports leagues. In addition, their respective college sports draw many fans. However, soccer has not taken off in the same way as the other four, and this is due to a lack of devoted fans.

Within college sports in 2019, Syracuse University averaged 21,992 fans per men's basketball game; in 2010, Louisiana State University averaged 10,673 fans per baseball game; in the 2019–20 season, the University of North Dakota averaged 11,300 games per men's ice hockey game; and in 2019, the University of Michigan averaged 111,459 fans per football game.[202] All four of these statistics represent the average attendance

202 "NCAA Men's Basketball Attendance," NCAA, accessed July 14, 2020; "Baseball Attendance," NCAA, accessed July 14, 2020; "2021 Men's Ice Hockey Records," NCAA, accessed July 14, 2020; "NCAA Football Attendance," NCAA, accessed July 14, 2020.

of each sport at the college with the team with the highest average attendance for that specific sport.

The men's college soccer team that averages the most attendance, however, is the University of Maryland, with only 2311 people per game.[203] For comparison, the average attendance at a Vanarama National League (fifth tier of English football) game before the end of the 2019–20 season was just under twenty-two hundred fans.[204] Maryland, the highest attended team in American men's college soccer in terms of fan draw, has attendance comparable to that of teams playing non-league football in England. That contrasts sharply with the fact that in college basketball or football, it's not uncommon for players to go straight from their college teams into the highest level of the game.

On the professional level, the statistics are a little better. The average MLB game has 28,317 spectators.[205] The average NFL game has around 66,479 fans.[206] The NHL and NBA record roughly 17,423 and 17,794, respectively, in their most recent 2019–20 seasons, but their stats are unreliable. Since sports are played indoors and in winter, they can only be played in fully functioning buildings rather than the outdoor fields and diamonds of baseball, American football, and soccer.[207]

---

203 "2020 Men's Soccer Record Book," NCAA, accessed July 14, 2020.

204 "Vanarama National League – Average Attendance – Home Matches," Football Web Pages, accessed July 14, 2020.

205 "MLB Attendance Report 2019," ESPN, accessed July 14, 2020.

206 "NFL Attendance 2019," ESPN, accessed July 14, 2020.

207 "NHL Attendance Report 2019-2020," ESPN, accessed July 14, 2020; "NBA Attendance Report – 2020," ESPN, accessed July 14, 2020.

Major League Soccer records only 21,310 people per game, which puts them significantly lower than the two other outdoor sports.[208]

Men's basketball and football are the two most popular college sports. For the annual NCAA basketball tournament in the spring of 2019, the sixty-seven games averaged over ten million viewers per game.[209] The 2019–20 NCAA football playoffs, which, by comparison, only include three games as opposed to sixty-seven, averaged 23.4 million viewers.[210]

The 2019 NCAA Football Championship had roughly 27.3 million viewers.[211] The 2018 FIFA World Cup Championship between Croatia and France had 1.12 billion viewers.[212] To put that in perspective, about 8.25 percent of the United States population of 331 million viewed the NCAA Football National Championship, while roughly 14.68 percent of the world's 7.6 billion people viewed the 2018 FIFA World Cup Final.[213] That means the engagement in the World Cup was roughly double that of the NCAA Football Championship... for the entire world.

---

208 "2019 MLS Attendance," Soccer Stadium Digest, accessed July 14, 2020.

209 Christina Gough, NCAA March Madness basketball tournament average TV viewership from 2013 to 2019, distributed by Statista.

210 "2019-20 Report: Amazing College Football Popularity Highlighted by Impressive Ratings and Attendance Data," *National Football Foundation*, May 28, 2020.

211 Ibid.

212 "More than half the world watched record-breaking 2018 World Cup," FIFA.com, December 21, 2018.

213 "World Population by Year," Worldometer, accessed July 15, 2020; "Population by Country (2020)," Worldometer, accessed July 15, 2020.

The primary argument against this point would be that comparing college football and international soccer is like comparing apples and oranges, which is a valid complaint. The most accurate comparison to make between sports is comparing the same ones across country lines. The best way to do this throughout most of Europe is to compare different soccer leagues, measuring which country has the most engagement and how well the league runs. This is because they are such similar systems and all operate under a universal international law established by FIFA, except MLS, which violates a few FIFA requirements. For example, MLS has no concept of relegation.

A good way to compare a mainstream American sport to a mainstream European sport is to make steady comparisons between second tier sports in both regions.

***

The Turkish Airlines EuroLeague, which is the UEFA Champions League of European basketball, has eighteen teams from ten countries who play EuroLeague during the week and domestic league on weekends, much like soccer.[214] The EuroLeague is the most popular professional basketball league outside of the United States, with the most popular basketball league in the world being the National Basketball Association (NBA) by far the most popular professional basketball league in the world based in North America—with teams in the United States and Canada. Currently,

214 "EuroLeague 2020-21 Teams," Turkish Airlines EuroLeague, accessed July 15, 2020.

twenty-nine of the thirty teams are based in the United States. The Toronto Raptors, however—the only Canadian team in the league—were crowned champions in 2019.

The EuroLeague has been in action since 2000. Before the creation of the EuroLeague, FIBA, the International Basketball Federation, regulated the continental league since its founding in 1958. In 2000, the organization, as well as operators of the league, changed. FIBA lost their control of the European league. They have, however, maintained control of the FIBA World Cup and the basketball portion of the Summer Olympics.[215]

The largest difference between the two leagues is money.

The NBA and the teams affiliated with the NBA make more money than the Euroleague and the Euroleague teams, which is primarily because of the disparity of support. While both leagues attract a sustainable amount of support from their population pool, the NBA is the superior of the two leagues. The NBA is more successful for five key reasons: (1) They have money, which attracts (2) talent, which (3) makes the games more exciting to watch, which leads to (4) longevity of great players on the same team, which leads to (5) long-term team buy-in.

This cycle also explains why soccer is more popular in Europe. Talented stars from both sports, such as Lebron James or Christiano Ronaldo do move around, but they are

215 Sebastian Komianos, "FIBA AND EUROPEAN BASKETBALL – STATUS RELATIONSHIP: IT'S COMPLICATED," *CourtSide Diaries*, June 10, 2016.

highly-sought-after medium-term investments for teams such as the Miami Heat or Real Madrid. A great American soccer player in MLS, on the other hand, is likely to switch continents to max out potential and earnings in Europe. Similarly, a EuroLeague star is likely to make the opposite switch to the United States for identical reasons.

***

Another reason the NBA flourishes where the EuroLeague fails is that they have more homegrown talent and are supported by the nature of the game in the country. As basketball is to the United States, where within urban centers around the country you would be hard-pressed to find an empty court, soccer is to Europe. Playing soccer in Europe at the local pitch or street arena is more prevalent than playing basketball or football at your neighborhood park or in your driveway—whereas the opposite is true in the United States. In a 2013 study, ESPN found that the number of youths participating in basketball was about double that of American youth participating in soccer.[216]

This illustrates the problems with soccer in the United States. The United States has consistently failed to inspire young people to get excited about soccer. Thus, fewer kids and teens play soccer than other sports—particularly basketball and football—and the U.S. paid the price, as they failed to even qualify for the last World Cup. As the United States continues to flounder within the realm of men's soccer, they

216 Bruce Kelley and Carl Carchia, "'Hey, data data — swing!'" *ESPN*, July 11, 2013.

increasingly rely on the exceptions to the exclusive youth system, like Christian Pulisic, who takes an alternate path to success. This could be fixed by making the path to success from the United States more accessible.

"We put them in tryout and team situations before they are psychologically and emotionally ready," said Chris Moore, chief executive officer of the US Youth Soccer Association, in an interview with *Cape Charles Mirror* in 2018. "So, if you can't make a travel team, some kids may say, 'What's the point,' and quit playing altogether."[216]

That is not the only reason kids fall away from the sport, however. In the same interview, Ryan Mooney, U.S. Soccer Federation's Chief Soccer Officer, said that increasing participation is important to increasing the quality of the sport, which is very true, whether it be at the international level or the domestic level. As the talent pool grows, so too does the skill of the top talent.[217]

Since Mooney acknowledged the need for increased participation, why does the U.S. continue to exclude people? Why do players continue to be shunned by USA Soccer? The answer is simple.

Money.

It's impossible to be deeply involved in soccer in the United States because unlike basketball or football, the sport does

---

217 Wayne Creed, "Youths are abandoning soccer in the US," *Cape Charles Mirror*, July 22, 2018.

not bring the community together. The sport does not inspire. The sport merely consolidates funds so that people may benefit from other's desires to really experience the sport.

KEY TAKEAWAYS:

- Soccer is vastly underperforming in the U.S., both domestically and on the international level, with the United States Men's National Team.
- MLS is to soccer as the EuroLeague is to basketball—respected, but by no means the pinnacle of the sport, simply a step along the way.
- One of America's most crippling challenges is that they fail to develop youth soccer culture.

CHAPTER 14

CHRISTIAN PULISIC

Christian Pulisic was born in Hershey, Pennsylvania in 1998.

Pulisic is hands down the American with the most exciting career yet. "Americans now finally—*finally!*—have a player capable of making an indelible mark on the world's game," wrote George Dohrmann, a consistent contributor for *Sports Illustrated,* in a 2017 *Bleacher Report* article.[218] The best part is Pulisic is still very young.

This may come as a shock to many people who aren't familiar with his age because he's not only been playing but starting in the United States Men's National Team's senior squad since 2016. Since his initial induction into the squad, he has been an integral part of the team. His name has also been discussed in Europe as one of the top young talents in the German Bundesliga until his transfer to Chelsea of the English Premier League at the beginning of the 2019–20 season. He is the most well-known American to ever play in Europe.

218 George Dohrmann, "The Christian Pulisic Blueprint," *Bleacher Report,* June 7, 2017.

His story, sadly, is unique among American players who aspire to be world-class soccer players, and it's not for lack of talent. In fact, Pulisic himself wrote in the Players' Tribune following the U.S. Men's National Team failure to reach the 2018 World Cup, "I think it's important to make clear, you know, that the problem with American Soccer...It isn't talent."[219]

Pulisic has played soccer for as long as he can remember. "I always had a soccer ball with me. I could never stop. As young as I could remember, my dad was always throwing a soccer ball at me," he said. His parents were formative in the development and execution of his goals. Having both played at George Mason University, his parents were extremely supportive of his goals to achieve soccer excellence as well.[220]

As a boy, Pulisic was a bit of a runt. He was short and skinny, which proved especially difficult as he played with kids many years older than he was. By age fourteen, he was called up to the United States' under-17 team.[221]

While playing for that squad, he met a challenge in the form of the under-seventeen Brazil team. Brazilians are world-renowned for their footballing skills, and Brazil has produced some of the best players in the world. Some of

---

219 "U.S. Soccer star Christian Pulisic speaks out on failure to qualify for World Cup," *USA Today*, November 13, 2017.

220 Jeff Carlisle, "U.S. starlet Christian Pulisic eager to prove himself at Borussia Dortmund," *ESPN*, 30 January 2015.

221 *VICE Sports*, "Das American: Christian Pulisic's Spectacular Rise," November 9, 2016, video, 15:03.

their most formidable productions include Pelé, arguably the best player ever; the original Ronaldo, who dominated the 1990s and 2000s with his international partner Ronaldinho—who could perform magic with his footwork; and the modern-day Neymar Jr., who has inspired millions of young players around the world through his skill with the ball.[222]

Pulisic took on this challenge easily, and his American side defeated the Brazilians 4–1 in the under-seventeen Nike International Showcase. After his MVP performance in the thrashing of the youth of one of the world's footballing superpowers, he caught the eyes of some scouts from Europe.[223]

After having his choice of which internationally renowned club to join, he decided on Borussia Dortmund from Dortmund, Germany. Borussia Dortmund has an international reputation for grooming young talent and giving them in-game experience at a young age. This reputation is arguably unmatched by any other team of their caliber. Some additional young talent to come through their side in the recent past includes Jadon Sancho and Achraf Hakimi. At just fifteen, Pulisic made a tremendous decision to uproot his entire life. He moved to a foreign country with a foreign language for the sake of the sport he loved.[224]

By 2015, and at age sixteen, Pulisic broke into the Dortmund first team, where he scored two goals in his first season as the Bundesliga's youngest player ever to accomplish such a

---

222 Ibid.

223 Ibid.

224 Ibid.

feat. The atmosphere for his first goal was unimaginable. The seething golden-and-black-dressed crowd chanting ceaselessly as he netted his first-ever goal at just seventeen years and 212 days of age in a 3–0 home win against Hamburg.[225]

His meteoric rise continued as his playtime shot up the following season. He played twenty-nine games, more than tripling his appearances the season before, and netted three more goals and assisted in six. As his statistics improved, he became a household name in America. By the time he was nineteen, he had become the youngest American player ever to score for the United States Men's National Team at eighteen and a half, and by twenty-one, he was the youngest player to ever captain the team.[226]

After two more outstanding seasons with Dortmund, where he netted eight more goals and assisted nine, he received a transfer to the most popular soccer league in the United States, the English Premier League.

TRANSFERS EXPLAINED:

Many Americans who don't follow soccer, but follow American sports like basketball, baseball, or American football, have a hard time understanding how transfers work within soccer. Three big concepts within soccer are very different from American sports.

---

225 Ibid.

226 Ibid; "Christian Pulisic, 20, becomes youngest in modern era to captain U.S. men's national team in 1-0 loss to Italy," *Chicago Tribune*, November 20, 2018.

First, the breadth of the sport means there are hundreds of professional leagues around the world, let alone teams. Within that statistic, some teams and leagues are less acknowledged and lower grossing than others, but the scale is much higher than comparable U.S.-centric sports.

The U.S. National Football League (NFL) allows a maximum of fifty-three players for a roster. With thirty-two teams in the NFL, this equates to 1,696 players across the entire league.[227] The U.S. National Basketball Association (NBA) permits fifteen players on an NBA roster, and there are only thirty teams, which means there are only 450 professional basketball players in the top division.[228] That metric does not quantify the number of G League players across the country.

U.S. Major League Baseball (MLB) allows for twenty-five players for the active roster of a team and forty for the extended roster.[229] This means the entire league has 800 active players, with an additional 480 players in the reserves. MLB, like the NBA, does have lower-level, developmental leagues, which field an additional 6050 to 6200 players, but for the sake of comparison, these lower-level teams have been omitted from the statistic.[230]

The top five soccer leagues in the world are at comparable levels to the aforementioned American leagues of their

227 Marc Lillibridge, "The Anatomy of a 53-Man Roster in the NFL," *Bleacher Report*, May 16, 2013.

228 Austin Kent, "CBA Explained: NBA Roster Size Limits," *SLAM*, August 16, 2019.

229 "MLB Rosters 2020," Lineups, accessed July 15, 2020.

230 231. J.J. Cooper, "Ask BA: How Many Players Are in Each Organization?" *Baseball America*, August 21, 2018.

respective sports. All contain their various lower leagues, which play similar roles in the sports hierarchy as the developmental leagues of American sports. Together, the leagues contain a much higher collective sum of players.

The English Premier League (EPL) contains about twenty-five players across twenty teams that are part of the first-team squad, which means that league has around 500 players. The French Ligue 1 has eighteen teams, which equates to 450 players. The German Bundesliga has eighteen teams as well, which means 450 more players. The Spanish Primera Division has twenty teams and 500 more players, and the last, but not least European league, the Italian Serie A, has twenty teams and another 500 players.

The sum of these leagues is about twenty-four hundred players across the main top-flight leagues in Europe, which is much more than any sport in America, and the extent of the lower leagues is so much broader than that of American Sports because there are so many more different and diverse leagues. England alone has four professional leagues and more than one hundred clubs that consider themselves full-time professional teams. This means English teams have a much harder time discerning young talent from their own pool of players, let alone the different systems that exist in almost every European country and throughout the world.

Another factor that contributes to the different systems is the relationship with lower league teams. In American sports, top teams in MLB or the NBA will have affiliated lower league teams. In soccer, most lower league clubs are independent.

There is no team system. The Kansas City Royals of Major League Baseball, for example, are affiliated with nine minor league baseball teams. This means they are the parent team to those nine teams. All the players contracted to the Kansas City Royals are distributed throughout the ten teams (including the Royals' team themselves). The Royals can organize and control the flow of players moving them from team to team based on skill level.[231]

Such a system is very rare in professional soccer. Some teams have second teams, such as FC Barcelona B, which is an offshoot of the world-class FC Barcelona, but clubs like this are the exception to the rule. Clubs also have youth systems that are functionally similar to minor league baseball. Youth teams will play against other youth teams of a similar age such as under-seventeens or under twenty-ones. The problem is that most teams don't have enough seventeen- or twenty-one-year-olds to provide their top prospects with the experience of playing with equally talented peers. Or, what if teams want their players playing with seasoned veterans who have experience and can serve as role models, but they aren't good enough to play in the first team yet?

The prevalent practice that has been established to give young players real playing time without risking losses on the big stage is known as loaning. Many professional teams will loan young players out to lower divisions, a lot of the time within their own country. Arsenal, for example, has twelve players

---

231 "Teams by MLB Affiliation," MLB, accessed July 15, 2020.

on loan as of January 2020, many of them young English players at lower tiers in England.[232]

The third and final reason soccer transfers are so difficult to comprehend for people familiar with the trading system of most American sports is that players in the soccer community are sold for price tags. The commonplace barter or swap present in American sports is extremely rare and unique in soccer. The most recent relevant example would be the January 2018 Manchester United-Arsenal swap of Alexis Sanchez and Henrikh Mkhitarian.

Apart from extremely rare examples like that one, transfers are done by teams purchasing the right to sign players to contracts from other teams. After the price has been agreed upon, the player signs a contract with the new team. Some things that might dissuade them from doing so would be the potential of moving to a new city, which might include immigrating and even learning a new language (Like Pulisic moving to Dortmund where German is spoken). Another potential dissuasion factor would be a pay cut. After negotiating the terms with the new club, the transfer is concluded and the club losing the player is paid the fee agreed upon.

A transfer is when one player moves to another club. This involves the acquiring club giving money to the player's current club for the right to negotiate with a player under contract. When the player is not under contract with another club, then the transfer is referred to as "free." Following the

---

232 "Arsenal Squad: Men Information & Details," Arsenal.com, accessed January 1, 2020.

exchange of this transfer fee, the acquiring club typically inherits a contract. Often, this requires the acquiring company to negotiate the contract.

Based on a simple understanding of economics, this concept of transfers is much more efficient than the American trading system. Obviously, an established currency leads to more order and efficiency within an economy than the old-fashioned bartering system used in ancient civilizations that predated the existence of currency. Why are some of the most advanced professional sports leagues in the world still using an economic system comparable to that of the ancient Mesopotamians?

***

Before Pulisic secured his move to Chelsea, one of the best clubs in England and in the world, the highest fee paid by any club for an American was around $22 million. Wolfsburg paid that for John Brooks, an American defender who they acquired from Hertha Berlin in 2017. Chelsea paid almost $73 million in a record-shattering transfer for Pulisic in 2019. He secured a 5.5-year, $72.5-million deal with the club.[233]

As the sport continues to grow in the United States, his story will provide immense inspiration to young Americans around the country aspiring to share in his glory. His entrance onto the English football scene will also provide an example of what Americans have to offer to the Premier

---

233 "Future of Christian Pulisic: The Most Expensive American Soccer Player Ever," *The Sideline Observer*, January 18, 2019.

League because no American has ever dominated that league in the way he has the potential to do.

It's much too soon to tell how successful he will be at Chelsea, but early indicators suggest he has the potential to be a world-beater. He has the potential to be the soccer poster-boy American soccer so desperately needs. He also has the potential to be a one-and-done in the grand scheme of American soccer. It's possible he will be amazing but that no one will follow in his footsteps. U.S. Soccer must acknowledge his success and attempt to use it as leverage over the next five to ten years to establish themselves as a nation accustomed to having many top quality players in not only the English Premier League but also the other top leagues in Europe.

However, many in the U.S. believe Americans should only play in the American domestic league. This belief is wrongheaded because the quality of play and the available salary for American players is much greater in Europe than in MLS. Thus, American players in Europe illustrate the country's growth in soccer, and today, unlike in 1998 when Pulisic was born, many more Americans have a chance to play in top European Leagues.

KEY TAKEAWAYS:

- Christian Pulisic has the potential to not only be the best American soccer player of all time but one of the best in the world ever.

- Pulisic's story is a little different than that of many other American soccer players, due to his early entry into the European leagues.
- Soccer transfers are very different from trading systems prevalent in American sports.
- Instead of having a series of affiliate teams, it's much more common for soccer clubs to engage in loan deals with lower league teams.

CHAPTER 15

PAY-TO-PLAY

The former First Lady of the United States, Michelle Obama, has addressed a problem that faces American soccer in some of her speeches. "Our greatness has always come from people who expect nothing and take nothing for granted," she said in her commencement speech for the City College of New York in 2016.[234]

While First Lady Obama wasn't speaking about soccer, her words only further exposed the idea that the people of the United States of America still face tremendous inequalities. These inequalities continue to resonate within the American world of soccer.

***

The trajectory of American soccer has a wide swath of endings. To illustrate just a few, here are three stories that generalize and explain three different outcomes.

---

234 "Commencement Address by First Lady Michelle Obama," The City College of New York, accessed July 16, 2020.

***

The first story is about Kelly, an upper-middle-class white girl from a Minneapolis suburb, who started playing soccer for her private Catholic school's youth team when she was five years old. Growing up, she lived with her parents and her little brother. Every other girl on Kelly's team was white, Christian, and attended her private school. Kelly's competition was a collection of other small private school teams composed of girls with similar demographics. As she grew up, she developed an affinity for soccer. By twelve, she was on a selective club team, paying $3,000 a year to be one of eighteen girls traveling around the country for tournaments in Kansas City, Chicago, and other regional hubs, with the occasional trip to Las Vegas or Ft. Lauderdale—every weekend, a different city. Kelly's family paid an additional $3,000 a year just to get her to her games around the country, hoping she might be seen by a college scout or two.

After starting high school, she tried out for her high school's team and made the varsity team during her freshman year. Her soccer talent progressed consistently, and she excelled against her select competition. By the time she was a junior, she was attracting scouts from local colleges. Kelly is now a senior in high school with offers ranging from local schools such as the University of St. Thomas to schools with more funding and more skill, such as the University of North Carolina and the University of Michigan.

***

The next story is about a different soccer experience in the United States. Adrian lived with his two older brothers and three younger sisters in the Bronx, where he spoke Spanish at home and English at school. Both of his parents are first-generation Guatemalan immigrants fluent in Spanish but with lackluster English skills. His dad works in a factory putting cranes together, and his mom works as a part-time lunch lady at a local public elementary school along with her full-time job as a maid in the more affluent areas of New York City.

Adrian has grown up playing soccer all his life. He juggled in the streets and played games on his neighborhood basketball court with the rest of the kids on his block. Like most, his parents can't afford to pay $3,000 just for him to play organized soccer. Instead, he plays informal soccer with his friends and family in the streets. After improving his touch and individual skill completely within his community, Adrian made the varsity team at his local public high school, which was composed entirely of kids who, like he, grew up playing on the streets. After competing within the local high school system for four years, Adrian is about to join the workforce because he could not get a scholarship offer from any of the colleges interested in signing him, despite his obvious knack for the game.

Unlike Kelly, Adrian was never given the opportunity to play under the close watch of college scouts from all around the country in Fort Lauderdale or Las Vegas. He was never given the opportunity to go to the scouts but always had to wait for them to find him, and like many American soccer players, they never did.

***

While the third story is not set in America, it does illustrate a common situation in the realm of world football.

The story is about Edson, who grew up in the Bauru in the State of Sao Paulo in Brazil, where he experienced extreme poverty. Growing up, he couldn't even afford a ball. Instead, he was forced to improvise and use a sock stuffed with a newspaper in order to learn the game. He was forced to play for local youth teams because he, like Adrian, was unable to afford to play for competitive traveling teams. Edson, however, led his team, Bauru Athletic Club Juniors, to two state titles. Like Adrian, the idea of college was off the table. If he couldn't afford a soccer ball, how would he ever afford a degree?

Ultimately, after his success with his local team, Edson secured a move to Santos, a rather successful Brazilian soccer team. After demonstrating an extremely high level of talent, he did eventually find his way into American soccer, signing for a professional team in New York.

***

Kelly and Adrian's stories are not uncommon in American soccer. Many young people of all backgrounds grow up playing soccer and loving the game. In the 2018 season, three million young people participated in soccer in the United States.[235] Many talented young players like Adrian slip

235 "Who is US Youth Soccer?" US Youth Soccer, accessed July 16, 2020.

through the cracks, while some of the other talented young people, like Kelly, can use soccer to get an athletic scholarship to help ease the financial burdens of college.

The problem with American soccer is that the system heavily favors people like Kelly over people like Adrian despite their comparable talent against peers. Higher-class, generally white, people are much more likely to succeed in American soccer because they are much more likely to be given opportunities like those presented to Kelly. While both Kelly and Adrian are fictional people, they represent many young people around the United States who experience varying levels of opportunity or lack thereof. Edson's story, however, is about someone who really lived and played soccer.

Edson Arantes do Nascimento was born in Brazil in 1940. While playing in school, he picked up the nickname that stuck with him the rest of his life, Pelé.[236]

Many have addressed the disparity between the wealthy and the poor before to help elevate those who have been trodden on by society. American soccer doesn't need to close this gap to be more equal. It needs to close this gap because it's the reason American soccer consistently falls short. While closing the gap for equality's sake would be an amazing feat, it would also greatly increase the quality of not only the national team but also Major League Soccer and other leagues in the United States, which would produce more revenue for U.S. Soccer and those leagues.

---

236 Biography.com Editors, "Pelé Biography," *A&E Television Networks*, updated July 16, 2019.

"I think sometimes we have to be courageous with ourselves and admit when we have a problem," said Nick Lusson, the director of NorCal Premier Soccer Foundation, a league founded to strive for diversity in the San Francisco area, when discussing inclusion issues in American soccer.[237]

The United States needs to have the courage to accept the problems at the roots of American soccer. The highest level of the sport lacks diversity, and we need to recognize this for what it is. It is a problem but one we can fix. We have the organization and the funding to make it possible for kids who do not have Kelly's advantage to build their talent and learn the game in a setting that provides them a future.

***

Soccer doesn't flourish in a privileged environment. Much like Pelé, many of the world's greatest players have risen out of adversity. Perhaps one of the greatest examples of players from this background is Carlos Tevez. He is widely recognizable from the third-degree burns he received in his childhood. Tevez, one of the greatest Argentinian soccer players to ever play, has recounted childhood stories of his impoverished violence and drug-ridden town.[238] His father was actually kidnapped and ransomed back to him after he became an internationally renowned player.[239]

---

237 Les Carpenter, "'It's only working for the white kids': American soccer's diversity problem," *The Guardian*, June 1, 2016.

238 *GOALSIDE!*, "The Tragic Story of Carlos Tevez," August 25, 2019, video, 10:01.

239 Adam Crafton, "Carlos Tevez's father freed after being held for eight hours by kidnappers in Argentina," *Daily Mail*, July 29, 2014.

Carlos Alberto Martinez Tevez was born in 1984 in the crime-ridden Fuerte Apache district of Ciudadela, Argentina. The town is located on the outskirts of Buenos Aires, the nation's capital. His parents were unfit to raise him due to drug addiction, so he was raised by his aunt and uncle. His living conditions were horrendous.[240]

"We didn't have football boots, and we used a broken tennis ball instead of a football. I didn't use a proper ball until I was eleven," he recalled in an interview with *Daily Mail* in 2011.[241]

After sustaining third-degree burns from an accident involving boiling water and having a two-month recovery at a very young age, Tevez fell in love with the sport.[242]

"Street football is the greatest thing in the world. There is just you and your friends against the rest," he said in the same 2011 interview.[243]

In football, Tevez met one of his best childhood friends, Dario Coronel, who he went to school with in Ciudadela. Coronel's story is not that different from Tevez's, but with a different ending. Coronel was, if possible, more naturally talented at the game than Tevez, but by sixteen they had taken different paths. Tevez had dedicated his life to soccer, and his passion was playing for Boca Juniors, one of the

240 *GOALSIDE!* "The Tragic Story of Carlos Tevez."

241 Alex Kay, "Down Carlito's Way: Carlos Tevez on his terrifying neighbourhood, how he plans to help it, and his future," *Daily Mail*, June 9, 2011.

242 Ibid.

243 Ibid.

best teams in Argentinian soccer. Coronel had slipped into a spiral of drugs and gang violence. By seventeen, when Tevez was playing in the first division of Argentinian soccer, his friend was being pursued by the police, and rather than face them, he chose to take his own life.[244]

Tevez went on to have one of the greatest careers in the history of Argentina. By 2004, when he was twenty, he received the call up to the national team, where he scored sixteen goals during his first season—the most in international football. Before long, he was scoring goals in the topflight of the Brazilian league, where he racked up thirty goals in one season. Tevez's talent soon earned him a move to heights he never dreamed of. In 2006, Carlos Tevez joined West Ham United Football Club, located in the heart of London in the United Kingdom.[245]

"As a kid, I would never have imagined I would live in England for four years," he said.[246]

"I am very happy and contented that my daughter is growing up in a country as developed as this one," said Tevez in 2010.[247]

After his emergence from the South American barrios, Tevez's rise was explosive. Within a year of joining West Ham, he had secured a loan move to the football giants Manchester

---

244 *GOALSIDE!* "The Tragic Story of Carlos Tevez."

245 Ibid.

246 Sid Lowe, "Carlos Tevez launches explosive attack on 'boot-licking moron' Gary Neville," *The Guardian*, January 21, 2010.

247 Ibid.

United. However, before finally signing a long-term contract, he jetted from one Manchester team to another, joining the Red Devil's bitter rivals, Manchester City. At Manchester City, he propelled himself into the record books once again by leading the club to their first-ever Premier League title in 2012.[248]

His success and his desire to leave Manchester City again earned him a transfer to another European giant, this time in Italy. In 2013, Tevez joined Juventas, the best team in Italian soccer. After an unhappy and unsuccessful stint in the Chinese Superleague, Tevez returned to his beloved boyhood club, which had initially propelled him into the limelight.[249]

Tevez's story is not unique. Many other players have succeeded as Americans would say "against the odds," but in reality, it's much more common for professional soccer players to have used soccer to escape poverty than to have used wealth to enter soccer. The only odds they are defying is the extreme unlikeliness that they will be talented enough to play professional soccer in the first place.

While his story is riddled with more sadness and adversity than most, the basics of growing up playing on the streets and catching a break at a young age are a common backstory for many professional footballers. Many more footballers experience the hardships that Adrian, or Tevez, or Pelé had to overcome to rise to the level where they are. Kelly's story is a much less common feat, and the idea of manufacturing

---

248 *GOALSIDE!* "The Tragic Story of Carlos Tevez."

249 Ibid.

soccer the way the pay-to-play system orchestrates is an unorthodox method. Most great players are made in the streets, or in other informal settings, not through consistent organized practice from a young age.

The solution is simple. To provide a footballing experience to all, and to follow the traditional path of development, the United States needs to make it possible for the Adrians of the country to get into the original elements of the sport at an earlier age despite their financial disadvantages.

To do this, localities should prioritize programs for under-privileged and immigrant communities. These should include access to resources, infrastructure, and quality coaching.

Resources include access to tournaments and select leagues, which are often expensive. It also includes money for equipment—balls, shoes, shin guards, and practice tools. The U.S. is too large physically to depend on a national organization to provide the resources necessary to promote broad access to the sport. Thus, it's up to local leaders to do this. And often, the selective clubs with travel teams are not the helpers but part of the problem and the benefactors of the inequality. They are the ones blocking access and resources from getting to the already underserved communities.

Infrastructure involves both indoor and outdoor fields. In many parts of the U.S., winters are cold, and the games and training require indoor facilities. Too often these resources are operated by or dominated by select teams and clubs. Thus, curating equal access to fields and facilities all year is critical for U.S. soccer to succeed. Infrastructure also includes organizational systems in place that make it possible for players and teams to transition to different skill levels without drastic cost increases.

Finally, the U.S. lacks quality coaches across the country. Select clubs can retain coaches with licenses because licenses are expensive to obtain. Licenses for coaches and referees should be free, or extremely inexpensive. Moreover, because more resources and more money are available from teams and clubs such as Kelly's, this creates a vicious cycle where the clubs can monopolize the time and energy of the coaches who also have the time to improve and become professional at their trade.

This triumvirate of disadvantages causes many players who excel from ages ten to thirteen to simply be lost. Creating a plan that can be implemented across the U.S. and operated and led by communities is critical for the success of the game in the U.S.

The best example of the success of such a system is that of Iceland. The island nation of just over 330,000 people managed to qualify for the 2018 FIFA World Cup in arguably the most competitive conference.[250] Their key to success involved all three of the aforementioned keys to American success. If we are to succeed, scaling up from the Iceland example and recreating it at the local level across the United States is the path to success for America.

---

250 "Iceland Population (2020)," Worldometer, accessed July 16, 2020.

KEY TAKEAWAYS:

- American soccer, like many other facets of America, is ridden with inequality. At the heart of this inequality is the pay-to-play system.
- Around the world, soccer thrives on the streets—in informal settings—which is the opposite of how it works in the United States.
- To succeed, American soccer needs to adapt to eliminate the gap in opportunity for young soccer players around the country by integrating access to resources, infrastructure, and coaching.

CHAPTER 16

THEORETICAL MESSI

Lionel Messi is arguably the best footballer in the world at the moment, potentially ever. If he is not currently the best player, then he is without a doubt in the top two. The only other player in the world who has a shot at claiming such a title is Christiano Ronaldo. Messi is a thirty-two-year-old Argentinian international who currently plays for FC Barcelona. Ronaldo is a thirty-five-year-old Portuguese footballer who currently plays for Juventas but had a long and prosperous career at both Real Madrid and Manchester United before transferring in 2018 to the Italian side.

While Ronaldo was at Real Madrid from 2009 to 2018, the two most dominant forwards on either side of one of the biggest rivalries in sports sparked tremendous debate over which of them is truly the world's best. Since 2008 when Christiano Ronaldo became the first of the two to win the *Ballon d'Or*, an award given to the year's best footballer across all leagues and competitions in Europe, the pair have split eleven of the last twelve trophies, Ronaldo possessing five and Messi, after his 2019 win, possessing six. Additionally, the pair are first and second all-time in receiving the award.[251]

As Messi and Ronaldo have gotten on in years, the pair has also ignited a debate over a much more interesting question because it can have a much more creative answer. Who will be the next Ronaldo or Messi after they are done? And where will that theoretical Messi come from? At this point, there is literally no telling. Soccer is the most diverse it has ever been and only shows signs of further diversifying.

***

Of the twenty-four top goal scorers in the 2018–19 English Premier League season, only 25 percent hailed from England. Of the remaining 75 percent, nine players were from the remainder of Europe, four from South America, three from Africa, and one player each from North America and Asia.[252]

The rest of the top leagues in Europe breaks down like this: 36.4 percent of the top goal scorers from either the English Premier League, the French Ligue 1, the Italian Serie A, the German Bundesliga, or the Spanish Primera Division hail from the same country that the league is based in. 32.8 percent of the top goal scorers in their league are foreigners in the country in which they play, but still hold some sort of European nationality. The remaining third of top scorers in

---

251 Sean Gallagher, "Ballon d'Or winners and the top 10 players from 2000 to 2019: From Lionel Messi and Cristiano Ronaldo to Michael Owen and Ronaldinho," *talkSPORT*, May 29, 2020.

252 "Premier League Stats – Goals," Premier League, accessed July 16, 2020.

the top leagues are from non-European nations. 16.8 percent of them are from South America, 11.7 percent of them are from Africa, 1.5 percent are from North America, and 0.7 percent came from Asia.[253]

Just under one-third of players in Europe's top leagues identify internationally for a team not even on the same continent, and this does not even account for the players who hold dual citizenship, such as Raheem Sterling, a Manchester City Forward who led the English front line in their fourth-place finish at the 2018 World Cup but was born in Kingston, Jamaica. His story is not unique: countless players who play for European clubs were born in other countries or were the children of immigrants to those European countries.

The stats presented above even further mask a considerable amount of diversity within the game.

The real message presented here is that European sports are more wide-open regarding country of origin than American sports. The NFL, which has the least diversity in terms of the players' country of origin in 2017 had only 2.56 percent foreign players.[254] The NBA had around 24 percent foreign-born players in 2019, with some big names such as Luka Doncic

253 Ibid, "Serie A 2018/2019 – Top Scorer," worldfootball.net, accessed July 16, 2020; "Ligue 1 2018/2019 – Top Scorer," worldfootball.net, accessed July 16, 2020; "Bundesliga 2018/2019 – Top Scorer," worldfootball.net, accessed July 16, 2020; "Primera División 2018/2019 – Top Scorer," worldfootball.net, accessed July 16, 2020.

254 Callum Borchers, "The NFL has the most protests. It is also the most American sports league," *The Washington Post*, October 13, 2017.

and Giannis Antetokounmpo, who were born in Ljubljana, Slovenia and Athens, Greece, respectively.[255]

The MLB had around 28.5 percent foreign-born players in 2018, the majority of which hailed from Latin America, especially the Caribbean and Central America.[256] The NHL is spread throughout Canada and the U.S. more than many other professional sports leagues, has teams in both countries, and has around 31.1 percent international players. However, only 8.5 percent of those players hail from a country outside of Scandinavia and Russia, and only one player hails from outside of Europe (Nathan Walker from Australia).[257] In MLS in 2019, only 42.2 percent of players were even eligible to play for the United States, let alone were born and raised in the United States.[258]

- NFL: 2.56 percent (2017)
- NBA: 24 percent (2019)
- MLB: 28.5 percent (2019)
- NHL: 31.1 percent (2019)
- MLS: 57.8 percent (2018)

The point is that compared to other top professional sports, soccer players come from all over the world, which means that while it seems probable that the next Messi will come

255 "NBA rosters feature 108 international players in 2019-20," *NBA*, October 22, 2019.

256 "MLB rosters feature 251 international players," *MLB*, March 29, 2019.

257 "Active NHL Players Totals by Nationality," QuantHockey, accessed July 16, 2020.

258 "MLS Players by Birthplace," *MLS*, March 7, 2019.

from a top footballing nation, that may not necessarily be the case.

***

The traditional top footballing nations in the world are Argentina, Brazil, England, France, Germany, Italy, Netherlands, Portugal, and Spain. Combined, the nine nations have roughly 606 million people, which is only 7.7 percent of the world population.[259] If taken into account that the theoretical Messi would now be a male between the ages of five and nineteen, their stats get even worse.

Based on population pyramids from 2019, there are roughly 57.42 million boys from the ages of five to nineteen in the nine countries.[260] That is only 5.8 percent of the 985.6 million boys of that age internationally.[261] Therefore, it seems illogical to assume that the countries with shrinking population growth—mainly the European countries other than Brazil and Argentina—will continue to produce the world's most elite footballers. This was evident in the Premier League last year. While there were more English players in the league than any other nationality, the top three goal scorers were from three different African nations.[262] Mohammed Salah from Egypt, Pierre-Emerick Aubameyang from Gabon, and Sadio Mane from Senegal

259 "Population by Country (2020)," Worldometer, accessed July 16, 2020.

260 "Demographics," Worldometer, accessed July 16, 2020.

261 Ibid.

262 "Premier League Players – Overview & Stats 2019/20 & Archive," Premier League, accessed July 16, 2020.

scored twenty-two goals each and tied for first as joint top scorers in 2019.[263]

This is not to say that eventually English football will be dominated by non- English people. English players will always make up the backbone of the English Premier League because teams can only fill out their roster with seventeen non-homegrown players. The stars are becoming increasingly less English though. And given that the theoretical Messi is only the star of world football, not representative of the entire demography of the sport, the next Messi will likely not come from a traditional nation.

So where will he come from?

***

The answer cannot be precisely calculated, but it can definitely be predicted through analysis. Reason would suggest that the next Messi will come from a country with a disproportionately high number of young people. The obvious answer would be Africa. The continent has more population growth, thus more young people per capita than any other continent, by a lot. Of the 1.3 billion Africans, 18.1 percent or 235.3 million fit the archetype for the theoretical Messi of a boy between the ages of five and nineteen. They have 23.9 percent of the world's male youth.[264]

263 "Premier League Stats – Goals," Premier League.

264 "Demographics," Worldometer.

While it seems much more likely that the next greatest soccer player would flourish in these circumstances, it's still possible that they might end up coming from Brazil, England, Germany, or any other established footballing nation, just less likely than it has ever been in the past. Obviously, the top countries might have a more established footballing infrastructure and culture. Thus, Africa, full of youthful potential, seems to have its own obstacles to overcome. Abdullahi Boru Halakhe wrote an opinion piece on the eve of the World Cup in 2018 commenting on these.

"Across Africa, young boys will be watching Mane, Salah, and other African superstars on TV and dreaming of being like them one day. For many, that dream will never be realized unless African football associations address corruption, poor governance, and inadequate commercial sponsorship of the domestic leagues," Halakhe said. While corruption will inhibit the development of the soccer infrastructure as a whole in Africa, it does not necessarily mean that the individuals in Africa won't be able to make it in Europe, or even in America in the future.[265]

***

There is always the outside chance that the theoretical Messi might not come from either location. So just how likely is it?

Africa, without a doubt, has the most formidable proportion of youth to select from when compared to their total

265 Abdullahi Boru Halakhe, "Is African football talent finally coming back to Africa?" *Al Jazeera*, June 27, 2018.

population, but Asia has the most youth, which is simply a product of their immense population. They have roughly 565.8 million young males.[266] That is 57.4 percent of the youth in the world.[267] Both continents, however, continue to fall into the pitfalls described by Halakhe.

The rest of Europe has about 32.2 million youths, which are even fewer than that of the established nations and about 3.3 percent of the total.[268]

The remainder of Latin America (essentially everything south of Texas in the Western Hemisphere) has roughly 46.5 million that fit the loose mold. That is still less than the established nations and only slightly better than the remainder of Europe, with 4.7 percent of the theoretical Messis.[269]

Northern America (the United States and Canada) has about 34.8 million theoretical Messis despite having the highest-grossing professional sports for four of the major sports (besides soccer). That is about 3.5 percent of the global total.[270]

Australia and New Zealand have a measly 2.88 million out of 30 million total people, and about .3 percent of the world total. Australia did qualify for the World Cup. It is true that Australia has a less competitive area of the world as part of the Asian Football Confederation, and has an advantage funding-wise compared to many of their competitors, but the

---

266 "Demographics," Worldometer.

267 Ibid.

268 Ibid.

269 Ibid.

270 Ibid.

United States faces similar circumstances, with only a little more competition and a much larger population advantage.

The remainder of Oceania has about 1.2 million male youths and make up roughly .1 percent of the world's male youth total.[271]

***

Therefore, we can conclude that soccer talent and population are not direct corollaries. The most densely populated regions, and the regions with the highest populations of young people, still don't perform to the extent that traditional nations do. This means soccer success is not completely random but follows the infrastructure, which is why the few have been dominating the many. Recent falls in domestic player ratios are only marginally due to declining population growth throughout Europe and are much more attributable to expanding access to soccer infrastructure.

The evidence for this can be observed plainly in Icelandic football. Iceland has only 34,600 individuals who fit the proposed description of the future Messi.[272] Not only that, but they also have only 1.2 percent of arable land in their country, which means the land is well suited for farming.[273] While it's not an exact science, most arable land is ideal for a soccer pitch, thus having a very small amount of arable land would correlate to having a low level of soccer pitches, which tend

---

271 Ibid.

272 Ibid.

273 "Iceland Arable Land 1961-2020," MacroTrends, accessed July 16, 2020.

to be good when constructing a team to challenge at the international level. Having a good infrastructure in the form of soccer pitches is an important part of growing talent. To get around this, the Iceland FA (KSI) had to intentionally confront the unfortunate problems they faced.

After the 2008 recession dubbed, the *kreppa* in Iceland, their sports took off. Despite their intense population disadvantage, they used their small size and isolation to their advantage. The isolated country filled its indoor pitches with countless professional soccer coaches, and these coaches contributed dramatically to advancing the game in Iceland. From a young age, all young people interested were presented with viable options for entering and maintaining association with the sport. They homed in on their youth and built cohesiveness with fellow players from the small population.[274]

***

In the context of the United States, which obviously is much larger and much more populated, we need to home in on our youth and develop them further with more cohesiveness and unification. Because we do not have a global population advantage in the same way China, India, or the young population of Africa would, the only way the theoretical Messi can be an American is if we apply Icelandic science and commit focused, concentrated efforts.

---

274 Jonny Cooper, "The story behind Iceland's assault on world football," *The Telegraph*, May 11, 2018.

My proposed solution is that through the development of a soccer infrastructure like that of Iceland, we need to remove the pay-to-play system and return the sport to a humanity-based level—by making soccer an activity for young people to organically enjoy, not a job at which they must succeed. After all, that is how soccer brings people together, not through money but through community and engagement.

For the United States to boost its chances of producing the next Messi, we need to develop our soccer infrastructure and make it possible for young people to remain with the sport. To produce a player capable of filling Messi's shoes, we must give all the youth a chance and build the chemistry necessary for success so that such a player is not disincentivized by the system. History has shown that it will not happen spontaneously; we have to take the measures necessary to build this ideal soccer ecosystem.

***

So how do we do this?

Iceland did three things that we could replicate. First, they built pitches—particularly indoor pitches. According to the BBC, Iceland has thirty full-size all-weather pitches.[275] This means they have an indoor pitch for about every ten thousand residents of the country.[276] Moreover, they have built hundreds of smaller training pitches to ensure younger

275 Joe Lynskey, "Iceland: How a country with 329,000 people reached Euro 2016," *BBC Sport*, November 15, 2015.

276 "Demographics," Worldometer.

children have access to the fields, not just older and senior clubs.[277]

To replicate this same strategy, a community such as Omaha would need to build eighty-eight full-size pitches. Omaha has only a handful, and most are multi-use facilities used primarily for American football fields. The situation in Omaha reflects the situation across the country. Compared to other footballing countries, the U.S. has far too few quality fields to foster the player who will grow into the next Messi.

The second Icelandic takeaway is that the quality of coach education is important because it leads to more competent coaches throughout all levels of the sport and, thus, better players. In Iceland, this permeates the entire age bracket with some top coaches working primarily with preteens and youth. In America, our select coaches rarely spend most of their time with the youngest members of their club. But more importantly, Iceland made teaching coaches the fundamentals of coaching a priority. That means every kid in Iceland has access to a trained and certified coach. In 2015, .26 percent, or 848 people in Iceland held coaching licenses of UEFA B license quality or higher; that's 1 out of every 388 people.[278] Prioritizing coaching is one way the U.S. can improve dramatically over the rest of world football.

Finally, Iceland exports their best players. Gylfi Sigurðsson, the best player in their 2018 World Cup squad, has played overseas since he was fifteen, when he was inducted into the

277 Lynskey, "Iceland."

278 Ibid.

Reading Youth setup. Over the next fifteen years, he would play for four top-flight clubs—three in England and one in Germany. Since joining the Premier League, he has made 274 appearances and scored sixty goals for Swansea City, Tottenham Hotspur, and Everton.[279]

The United States has done this to a lesser extent with players such as Christian Pulisic, but focusing on finding alternative paths for great high school players is important. Three big challenges include conflicting interests with club versus school teams, irregularity of season across the U.S., and a developmental program that tries to be centralized in an enormous country.

For the United States to fully acclimate themselves to the level of success world football demands, they, like Iceland, will have to make an intentional effort. This involves shifting the culture of the game to a more community-based activity, growing soccer infrastructure, with the development of both new facilities and better coaches, and giving players who do succeed an avenue for continued success that allows them to pursue the sport at the highest level once they outgrow the American system. If all these things are done, the next Messi might just be American.

KEY TAKEAWAYS:

- Soccer is the most diverse sport in the world, mostly because it's a global sport.

279 "Gylfi Sigurdsson – Detailed Stats," Transfermarkt, accessed July 16, 2020.

- There is no telling who the next best player in the world will be.
- The best avenue for America to pursue to produce the Theoretical Messi is to embrace the system Iceland has done on a much larger scale and throughout communities across the country.

CHAPTER 17

SHELDON GRIZZLE AND CHATTANOOGA FOOTBALL CLUB

In late 2019, I had the pleasure of sitting down with Sheldon Grizzle and hearing his firsthand account of how Chattanooga Football Club went from a dream of his to a real organization and soccer club. Most of the information in this chapter comes from that exclusive interview I had with him.

***

Grizzle is one of the founding members of Chattanooga Football Club, a club established in Chattanooga, Tennessee in 2009. He has been interested in soccer for as long as he can remember and grew up playing for his local team as a child. During high school, he played for his school team at a high level and set the scoring record for the state of Florida.

Naturally, he decided to play college soccer. He chose to play at a smaller school to balance his life. That school ended up being Covenant College, where he started all four years and ascended to the top of the all-time scoring list. After a career in college, he decided it would be in his best interest to get married and find an alternative profession than continue his soccer career after college with a professional team.

Grizzle never played professional soccer despite his high-level college performances, but he really wanted to keep going with the sport. He decided that coaching was the natural next step to pursue. Initially, he became an assistant coach at Covenant, his alma mater. Following success at Covenant, Grizzle sought a new expression for his soccer coaching, becoming a travel soccer coach. He enjoyed club coaching because it was a way to stay involved with the sport that had shaped his childhood. It was a natural outlet for him.

Eventually though, he decided coaching wasn't what he wanted to do with his life, and in 2006, he wrapped up his coaching career. But he wasn't done with soccer. He started throwing around the idea of a Chattanooga amateur soccer team. Initially, there was not a lot of traction. The main league at the time was the Premier Development League (PDL), which became the USL League Two, which is roughly the fourth tier on the pyramid of American soccer. But the numbers didn't make sense at the time. As time wore on, Grizzle put the idea on the back burner until his friend, Thomas Clark, approached him in early 2009.

***

Clark told Grizzle that a league had recently started a new conference in the Southeast. At the time, Clark played for a team in Birmingham, Alabama, which is about two hours away from Chattanooga and quite a long commute for Clark. His proposal to Grizzle would change the shape of Chattanooga soccer forever.

He proposed that they begin their own soccer team in Chattanooga. They had some mutual friends who were willing to help fund the nascent club, but they wanted to see a business plan. Clark didn't know how to write a business plan, but he was set on the team. Grizzle didn't know how to get the team started, but he knew how to write a business plan because he did that for a living at the time.

Two weeks later, Grizzle and Clark sat down with those mutual connections, who later became board members, to discuss the future of the team. Daryl Heald and Krue Brock loved the plan. They followed up a few days after Grizzle and Clark made their proposal and said they'd love to make it happen. That was in January 2009. By May, they had a team on the field where sixteen hundred people showed up to watch the first match in the history of Chattanooga FC.

"The reason Heald and Brock got so excited about it was the idea that soccer is the world's game, a sport that transcends culture, racial lines, and economic lines," said Grizzle.

Building local soccer culture is one of the most important missing pieces around the U.S. In Europe, clubs are city, town, or even neighborhood teams. The club is a big part of the cultural identity of many communities. Many clubs are owned and operated not by billionaires, but by local soccer lovers first. Major League Soccer operates in a way that contrasts sharply with that narrative. They have usurped control of soccer from the locals.

***

The best example of control being vested in the people rather than elite owners can be found in the German Bundesliga. The German League has a rule known as the 50+1 Rule, which essentially prohibits majority ownership of the club from falling into the hands of one group or entity. For a team to compete in the German topflight, fans must be the majority owners of the clubs.[280]

This rule and ensuing system make it impossible for teams to prioritize profits over the success of the team and the interests of the fans. While there are a few exceptions to the rule, including Wolfsburg and Bayer Leverkusen, which were founded in 1904 by the pharmaceutical company, Bayer, and in 1945 by the automobile company Volkswagen, respectively, the rule applies to the vast majority of clubs.[281]

Thus far, the rule has paid off for German football. The Bundesliga consistently averages more spectators per game than rival leagues.[282] And on the international level, the German National Team has qualified for the last eleven

280 "German soccer rules: 50+1 explained," Bundesliga, accessed July 16, 2020.

281 Ibid.

282 Pramesh Pudasaini, "Top 10 Sports Leagues with the Highest Attendance Per Game," *The Richest*, March 21, 2014.

continental and international competitions, including six World Cups and five Euros since 1998 when the rule was instigated.[283] Furthermore, since 1998, the German National team has been ranked on average around sixth in the world and fourth in Europe.[284]

In the twenty-two years since the rule came into play, the German National team has been very successful. They have reached the quarter-finals of the World Cup five times, the semi-finals four times, the finals twice, and won the cup once. During the same period in the Euros, they have reached the semifinals three times and the finals once.[285]

Domestically, the league is doing terrifically. Borussia Dortmund is the international leader in average attendance of just over eighty thousand people per game during the 2018–19 season. Bayern Munich, which has won the last seven Bundesliga titles, had the highest average percentage of seats filled in the 2018–19 season, selling out 100 percent of the 75-thousand capacity Allianz Arena.[286]

Borussia Dortmund CEO Hans-Joachim Watzke summed up the relationship between community and club pretty well in 2016, saying, "The German spectator traditionally has close ties with his club…and if he gets the feeling that he's no

283 "Germany National Team – Fixtures & Results 2020," worldfootball.net, accessed July 16, 2020.

284 "The FIFA/Coca-Cola World Ranking – Ranking Table," FIFA.com, accessed July 16, 2020.

285 "Germany National Team – Fixtures & Results 2020," worldfootball.net.

286 "German soccer rules: 50+1 explained," Bundesliga.

longer regarded as a fan but instead as a customer, we'll have a problem."[287]

Building a similar relationship between club and community in the United States could be the key to making soccer clubs an integral part of many community cultures around the United States and to turning around the success of the United States Men's National Team in world football.

***

Clearly, the 1,600 people who showed up to Chattanooga Football Club's first-ever game were deeply interested in the sport and wanted to see a local team play. Grizzle said, "This could be a great tool to bring diverse Chattanoogans together." And he was right. The city of just over 150,000 people, which is nowhere near large in terms of other cities in the United States, needed something along these lines to act as a centripetal force to pull the city together.

"From the very, very beginning, even before the beginning, we used soccer as a tool to build the community of Chattanooga," Grizzle went on to say.

There was no good example of what to do for Chattanooga FC. They were the groundbreaking pioneers who used their platform to create and empower a local soccer movement within the United States. Nobody who ran clubs did it to build community and reach the entire local population. There were no

287 Stephan Uersfeld, "Borussia Dortmund CEO: 'I don't want to see fans milked like in England,'" *ESPN*, November 16, 2016.

social impact aspects of MLS or MLS feeder leagues. People run clubs either because they love soccer or because professional sports tend to attract money. Sometimes they do it for both reasons. The Chattanooga FC founders could not find any clubs doing what they were doing. Either it wasn't going well enough for those clubs or clubs just weren't doing it.

Grizzle said, "I think we were definitely the first in the way of these community-driven clubs that have a social mission at its core, and soccer was the excuse to come together." For example, Chattanooga FC has helped build multiple turf fields in poorer parts of the community.

"Every club that's been founded since we came on the soccer scene, I know that they look at what we do and aspire to be something like Chattanooga Football Club," Grizzle noted. "If you can do it in Chattanooga, Tennessee, you can do it anywhere."

As the Southeast League continued to grow in skill and interest, they realized they couldn't keep putting local players on the field. This didn't mean they had to stray from their goal of community development. They could still have a social impact by using foreign players and out-of-state players. The real impacts were with their fans and across the youth and teen leagues in Chattanooga.

After a couple of seasons in the league, they had to begin using international players. Their primary source of these players was from the National Association of Intercollegiate Athletics (NAIA), Division II and Division III schools. For Division I schools, it just wasn't possible to get the players.

They had longer seasons. It was harder to get them to move to Chattanooga and almost impossible to get them playing for a club.

The first coach, Bill Elliot, had three decades of experience, and one of his primary skills was his ability to reach out to players around the country and around the world to play for Chattanooga FC. After a few years of this, the word got around that Chattanooga FC is a good place to play. People wanted to spend their summer there. This benefited the club because they leveraged this media and positive attention to recruit players.

Their roster truly included players from many different backgrounds. They had NAIA players such as Jaoa Costa from Truett McConnell University and Jordan Dunstan from Bryan College. They had Division II players like Juan Sanchez from Palm Beach Atlantic University and Soren Yuhaschek from the University of West Florida. They had past Division I athletes like Cameron Woodfin from East Tennessee State. They even had non-college players like Juan Hernandez, the Spanish midfielder who had previously played at Rocket City United and has been with the club for the past five years.

***

There are two chapters in Chattanooga Football history, with chapter one starting with the first eleven seasons, up until the end of 2019 season. They held their players with amateur contracts. They couldn't make pro contracts because of the legality of paying college athletes who were on school visas, as opposed to working visas, within the United States. All they could do was provide their college players with living expenses, health, food, and housing; there was no salary involved. That would have been illegal. The NPSL was semi-pro, so at times, players were tied down by professional contracts with other teams, but most of the teams employed similar methods as Chattanooga FC.

Thus begins the second chapter of the Chattanooga Football Club. Beginning in the 2020 season, Grizzle and the rest of the club have decided to join another league. The primary changes include no longer employing college student-athletes to play for them over the summer. They have also increased the length and skill level of their league and season. Before, they played a three-month season over the summer months. Now they play from late February through October. The primary reason for this is to turn the club from a three-month operation to a full-time commitment for players and professional staff. This requires a lot more attention and devotion.

As they started building the infrastructure and personnel for this full-time effort, they also sold shares of the club to the Chattanooga FC community. These shares were executed on a crowdfunding engine and represent the first attempt at community-based fundraising for an American soccer team.

The local ownership is similar to that of the Green Bay Packers of the NFL. The fundraising model represents another significant transformation from billionaire ownership to local community empowerment. Well, mostly local, I am a proud owner of Chattanooga FC.

***

The primary lesson Chattanooga FC shared with the world is that it's still possible to grow a club based around community engagement and inclusivity. Too many times, MLS has used their platform to build isolation, especially for smaller teams unable to compete on higher competitive levels because of financial barriers not present in other spheres of soccer like the English Football League and other top leagues and their systems in Europe.

KEY TAKEAWAYS:

- Chattanooga Football Club has pioneered a successful way forward for smaller clubs in the United States to not only begin but also to flourish in a difficult market. They have set an example for many other clubs that have followed in their footsteps.
- Chattanooga Football Club has at the heart of their mission the community aspect that makes soccer such a strong sport, a characteristic mostly lacking on the U.S. Soccer scene.
- It's entirely possible to run a successful club that does not compete within the same system or quite at the same level as Major League Soccer.

CHAPTER 18

DENNIS CROWLEY AND KINGSTON STOCKADE

Once again, I had the distinct pleasure of having a conversation with someone about their contribution to the world of American soccer. This time around, I spoke with Dennis Crowley about his role at Kingston Stockade.

***

Dennis Crowley is not only the founder of the popular search-and-discovery app Foursquare, but he is also the founder and chairman of the New York area soccer club, the Kingston Stockade.

Crowley started his first, pre-Foursquare, venture in 2003 with his classmate and cofounder, Alex Rainert. The two were grad students at New York University at the time. They wanted to delve into the intersections of mobile phones with location-based services and social software—resulting in their app, Dodgeball. Dodgeball was designed to function, as

Crowley put it, "like a marauder's map for texting." Crowley is referencing the magic map from the J. K. Rowling hit *Harry Potter* series. The premise of the map is that Harry and his comrades can see the location and track the movements of everyone on the school grounds.

The concept sounds a little creepy when phrased this way; however, Crowley's app was not a stalking app. The primary function was a location-based service geared toward sparking interactions between people based on geographic information.

Google found the idea attractive, and in 2005, they purchased the business. Crowley and Rainert found themselves employed by the tech supergiant. They came across a roadblock, however. After being enveloped by Google, they found that working with and through Google was extremely frustrating. They couldn't pursue what they had in mind effectively, and in 2007, the pair left Google to independently seek other sources of employment. By early 2009, Dodgeball had been discontinued.

After leaving Google and Dodgeball in 2007, Crowley decided to try again. This time, he would be in control and learn from his experience with Google.

In 2009, Crowley founded Foursquare with his new partner, Naveen Selvadurai. The pair capitalized on some brand-new technology that had come out since the creation of Dodgeball in 2003. Foursquare was founded with a similar premise as Dodgeball, but they geared their new venture toward an invention by Steve Jobs in 2007, the iPhone. Foursquare was the first company to popularize the idea of location-sharing, which can now be found throughout countless other location-based services.

"Foursquare is about understanding where phones are, where they have been, and where they might go in the future," said Crowley in late 2019.

According to a HubSpot blog, Foursquare increased platform adoption by 3,400 percent in 2010. And juiced by more than $300 million in venture capital, the New York City-based Foursquare has continued the pattern of strong growth throughout the 2010s.

Like Dodgeball before it, and its extension products Swarm and City Guide, Foursquare is fundamentally about building local networks that help people engage with their immediate surroundings. This locality based social media platform has been a significant driver of community-building efforts around the United States and the rest of the world.

***

Dennis Crowley is unlike Sheldon Grizzle in many respects. Crowley never played soccer growing up. He never played high school or college soccer. He was not a soccer fan as a kid or even a young adult. Only after college, when most of his friends were English Premier League fans, did he really discover the sport. The one thing the two do have in common, however, is that they are both founders of their respective clubs. While Grizzle founded Chattanooga FC, Crowley founded the Kingston Stockade.

After discovering the sport through his friends in the 2000s, he began to take an interest not only in the English Premier League that his friends enjoyed but also in the United States Men's National Team. In 2010, Crowley found his way to the World Cup in South Africa. At the same time, he began to play the game. He played primarily with his friends on a recreational, for-fun basis. But one day after playing they decided to get drinks, and he asked a question.

"What would have to happen for our club team to play the New York Red Bulls someday?" he inquired.

While this may have been a surface-level question he just spat out at a bar, it went somewhere. Over the next couple of months, they did some research and made some discoveries. Crowley made a call to Grizzle who had been at Chattanooga for several years and asked what it would take to replicate his success with Chattanooga in New York. The two spoke and in 2016, the dream was actualized, and the Kingston Stockade held their first tryouts.

The initial response to the development of the Hudson Valley team was not necessarily positive. Crowley received a lot of criticism. "Who's going to watch the games? Who's going to play for the team? Who's going to care?" people asked.

There were two moments when Crowley realized the gravity of the work he had put in. The first of which was when Stockade had their first tryouts and the doubts dissolved. Incredible players came out of nowhere. Crowley was in awe at the quality of players that had shown up for a shot to play for the club he had thought into existence. According to him, "That feeling was truly awesome."

"It is almost like these guys had been waiting for us to put an all-star Hudson Valley Squad together," he said.

The second moment was a couple of months later, when Kingston Stockade held their first friendly. He had invited a few friends to hang out at his house in Kingston as a warmup to the match. Afterward, they made their way to the stadium, where they watched without really paying attention as people paid their way through admission and into the game.

A minute or two after kickoff, something happened on the field to get the crowd riled up and they went wild. They were making so much noise that the coaches, the players, his friends, and Crowley himself looked up into the stands and realized that between eight hundred and nine hundred people had shown up for the inaugural match of the Kingston Stockade. Their mouths dropped. He was completely astounded and taken aback by what he had created in dreaming up the Kingston Stockade.

***

Now, every March, the Kingston Stockade holds their tryouts, where over two hundred skilled soccer players compete for thirty to thirty-five spots on the roster as the technical director and the coaching staff look on. After tryouts, the club plays a series of friendlies in April to prepare for a three-month-long league season in the National Professional Soccer League (NPSL) throughout May, June, and July.

Within the NPSL, they compete in the Northeast Region. Within the Northeast Region, they compete in the North Atlantic Conference. Last year, they finished third in a table, including New York Cosmos B, Brooklyn Italians, Hartford City FC, Rhode Island Reds FC, Greater Lowell Rough Diamonds, Boston City FC, and New York Athletic Club. The NPSL holds fourteen conferences across four regions, with ninety-two teams in all, coincidentally the same number of teams across the top four divisions of English football.[288]

Crowley holds a role as a board member of the NPSL, where he is in charge of observing and identifying where the NPSL fits within the U.S. soccer scene as a whole. In the context of Chattanooga FC, he has to ask the hard question: Where should they send teams that outgrow the NPSL?

In 2020, both Chattanooga FC and Detroit City FC would play in a new league completely disconnected from the NPSL. They both began to play in the National Independent Soccer Association (NISA) before the suspension of the season in the spring of 2020 due to public health risks posed by the COVID-19 pandemic. In a normal year, though, the season spans from March through October.[289]

"In the absence of promotion and relegation based on merit, there's a bunch of people working to align the leagues so that when a team does get a little too big, or too advanced, or just outgrows its existing league, it has a place to go," Crowley said. "There are a lot of people that recognize that the system

288 "Teams," NPSL, accessed July 16, 2020.

289 "Independent Cup," National Independent Soccer League, accessed July 16, 2020.

in the United States is unlike the systems elsewhere, I should say, anywhere else in the world."

Crowley does not completely agree with the way the United States has set up its system with the lack of relegation and promotion.

"Everywhere else in the world, you start at the bottom and you invest in your team. If your team does well, you move your way up," he said. "Here in the U.S., what you do is, if you have a team, you write a big check that goes to the league and you buy your way up."

Not only is the system of promotion in the United States backward compared to almost any other league in the country, but the theory of promotion in the United States also has three qualifications: (1) a "committed local ownership group"; (2) an "attractive" market with a history of supporting soccer; and (3) a "comprehensive stadium plan." These qualifications are in direct conflict with FIFA Rules. FIFA Article 9 dictates that "sporting merit" must be the "principal" factor. This essentially means that MLS and the feeder leagues that contribute teams to MLS based upon the three earlier provided qualities are in violation of the FIFA Statutes.[290]

"You should take the money and invest it in your team, and then your team should be awarded with promotion," Crowley said.

---

290 Terence D. Brennan, "Does U.S. Soccer's League Set-up Violate FIFA Rules?" *Medium*, February 9, 2017.

In terms of his other role as the chairman of Stockade in addition to being on the board for the NPSL, he aspires to follow in the footsteps of Grizzle and Chattanooga FC. "If you want to be an awesome lower-level club, just follow the Chattanooga playbook," Crowley said.

At Stockade, he has striven to make the club not only a productive part of the NPSL, and the Hudson Valley community but also a successful business. His annual goals with the club include trying to draw one-thousand-plus fans to each game of the season and to qualify for the U.S. Open Cup. Off the field, they include selling merchandise and inspiring the community to break even, or even make a profit from the ownership, and management of the club as a whole.

Even more fascinating is that Kingston Stockade has created a financial playbook for other clubs. They provide transparent monetary accounting of their revenue and expenses. Between Chattanooga FC and Kingston Stockade, the way soccer needs to grow in the United States is clear—community first, ground up—not top down.

While Stockade might be further back than Chattanooga in their development, both clubs have an important part to play in the sphere of the United States soccer scene. The two clubs play big roles in the NPSL and beyond as they expand and grow the sport as it could be, rather than how it has been in the United States.

By following their examples, and the examples of many others, the footballing scene in the U.S. will be steadily altered to further reflect its European roots.

KEY TAKEAWAYS:

- Kingston Stockade is another example of an American club that has devoted themselves to building community as part of their core mission.
- Dennis Crowley and the rest of Kingston Stockade were directly inspired by Chattanooga FC and Sheldon Grizzle.
- The lack of promotion and relegation in the United States is in direct conflict with FIFA regulations.
- The success of American football is rooted in growth from the ground up rather than from the top down.

CONCLUSION

The solution to the problem that has been outlined is not necessarily complex, but it's not an easy fix either.

American soccer, or more appropriately, Major League Soccer and the national teams, run a planned economy. Payroll is controlled, entry fees are set, and franchise costs are often shared. In short, the league and the organization are not market-based—not capitalistic.

Soccer in the United States should focus on three primary goals: (1) local growth of the game, (2) improved infrastructure to ensure access to fields, equipment, coaching, and referees, and (3) transitioning to market-based forces—including a system of promotion and relegation and community ownership throughout resembling the Chattanooga FC and Bundesliga models.

The solution and undeniable conclusion one must draw from the evidence is that instituting relegation and promotion in American soccer will stimulate the game. There will be infinitely more opportunities for younger players, and at much lower costs. Additionally, the increased competition would steadily increase soccer infrastructure in the U.S. as the game becomes more widespread and funding is more distributed across multiple leagues. Fandom will increase due to more possibilities and more interest, and MLS and American soccer will produce more money.

The transition to an open system will lead to the creation of more teams like Kingston Stockade at $125,000 rather than Nashville SC at $150 million, along with a $275 million publicly funded stadium. Nashville has not built the soccer community from the ground up. And so local players won't rise, and local teams won't flourish. Instead, Nashville will join a league that is well below the world's best, and as a result of the current system the league—and American soccer as a whole—will continue to stagnate and remain in their perch well below the best of the world.

The stagnation will be most evident once MLS reaches its cap—once they proceed to a point where it would be impossible to justify adding additional teams. The other four American sports leagues have all stopped around thirty, which is where they are soon headed. Once they reach this point, their business model fails.

Without the financial boost provided by tremendous buy-ins, and with a superior product readily available in the form of the Premier League or countless other leagues around the globe, how will Major League Soccer continue to be profitable? How do they make money when the great players rightly upgrade to better teams, and better leagues, just like Christian Pulisic?

They will need to provide some level of promotion and relegation to continue this excitement with every cycle as one team reaps the financial and esteemed benefits of being promoted to a higher level of soccer principally via merit. This will provide not only added excitement in accordance with FIFA regulations but also keep the league competitive and at its best, rather than making it possible for teams to perform poorly time and time again without any real incentive to improve. The increased competition would also bring increased profits, as a more interesting, more competitive league produces more money for the teams who build bigger fan bases, and the league that serves as an administrative and regulatory body over the league.

In the long run, promotion and relegation will produce better players, better teams, more engagement, better communities, and more money. But that money won't flow naturally to MLS owners' products. That is the problem. Thirty primarily white men sit atop the soccer monopoly sharing the spoils of the sport. This is the history of soccer and FIFA in a nutshell. The problem for these owners is that they are running out of line as MLS approaches the point at which they will have to rely on something besides ridiculously high franchise fees for profit.

***

MLS's primary argument against relegation is that the teams paid a formidable price to get where they are now. That is why I suggest that MLS close the league following the induction of the class of new teams joining in 2022. They will then establish that beginning in the 2030 season, they will use an established pyramid to promote and relegate the teams based on their performances within the league. This will drastically increase the fandom within those leagues, which are loosely followed not because of lack of talent, but because of a lack of relevance on the national scene.

It's inevitable that with the potential of reaching the top league through investment in the team rather than investment in the league, fans will gravitate toward the league as the drama and fandom become more personal and more intense.

The peak of this proposed pyramid would, of course, have to be Major League Soccer. They are without a doubt the most well-funded and secure league the United States has ever seen. I propose that every year, the bottom club from both the East and West division would be relegated. In addition, the second bottom club from each conference would play a home and an away leg to determine which of them would be relegated and which would remain in the league.

At this point, the second-tier league would be the USL Championship. The USL Championship, unlike the EFL Championship of England, is composed of thirty-five teams. To fully give each team a fair and feasible schedule, the league would be divided into two leagues based upon the geography in which the champion of each league would gain automatic promotion to MLS, replacing the lowest team of their respective region. The second and third place finishing clubs of both leagues would then be placed into a four-team, two-leg promotion bracket, the winner of which would be promoted. The two lowest finishing clubs from each of the geographically sorted leagues would then be removed from the USL

Championship and placed into the third tier, which is where things get messy.

The third tier is more difficult to demarcate because two unassociated leagues are currently at the same third tier level, so combining them into the same system would be extremely difficult. NISA and the USL League One are both roughly equivalent to the same skill quality. Additionally, both leagues are quite small, with eight teams and twelve teams, respectively. The first course of action would be to pump the two leagues with additional teams based on their performances in the first season of the new season from the extensive fourth tier, which would have over one hundred teams.

To do this, U.S. Soccer would have to begin preparation for the 2030 relegation-promotion date by starting the system of promotion and relegation at this level in 2028, 2027, or 2026, promoting between two and seven teams a year from the fourth tier while only relegating one from both of the third tier leagues. Doing this would keep the league competitive while also growing the size of the leagues.

After pumping both NISA and USL League One up to twenty teams, the leagues would then promote two each to the USL Championship, where they would dissociate based upon geography into the two leagues. The outright champion in each league would be promoted followed by the winner of a four-team, two-leg playoff in both leagues.

The three lowest-finishing teams from each league would then be relegated to the equivalent of the English Conference, and here would be the fourth tier and lower in American soccer. The fourth tier would have both the NPSL, which is composed of more than ninety teams divided into four regions—with a total of fourteen conferences, as well as the USL League Two, which has eighty-two teams divided into eight divisions—with nineteen total conferences.

The promotion process would be quite complex at this stage and would have to incorporate at least thirty-five teams. To make the numbers work, it would be most beneficial to include the thirteen next best performing teams to have forty-eight teams. The purpose of this would be to sort the teams into six groups of eight to fulfill the promotion needs of the third tier. The six groups would conduct individual one-leg playoffs, and the winner of each would earn a spot in the third tier.

An alternative would be to redistrict the leagues laid out above and redistribute the teams so that each league is geographically feasible. The ideal would be to have ten regional leagues with seventeen or eighteen teams each. Every year, the ten league winners would face off in a two-leg competition against their regional neighbor, and the winner of all five competitions would then be promoted. The sixth and final spot would serve as an opportunity to promote lower-league football.

The five champions that missed out on promotion as well as several other teams, the next best fifty-nine teams could be selected to run a knockout style tournament. The tournament, much like the college basketball tournament which takes place primarily in March, would be an exciting spectacle that would spark similar excitement within the American soccer community as well as bring money to local communities. The tournament could also be shrunk to have a smaller field, but a big fall tournament would be more exciting, especially if the winner was rewarded with induction into the football league.

Below the fourth tier, it's hard to qualify because there is no efficient way of sorting the seventeen USASA (United States Adult Soccer Association) states and regional leagues and the more than 250 UPSL (United Premier Soccer League) teams. In reality, the leagues are disorganized enough that they would probably have to work out their own systems to provide regional champions to challenge for positions in the already expansive fourth tier against the bottom finishing established fourth-tier team of their region.

Once again, the idea of a big tournament sounds appealing. There would be a series of open, regional tournaments with any team below the fourth tier eligible. Then the top teams would be promoted into the fourth tier according to the region in which they participated.

The system proposed above may have faults, but it's the most fully developed proposal of promotion and relegation that has been developed thus far. U.S. Soccer establishes relegation and promotion because this is the natural progression of the sport as articulated in FIFA Statute Article 9. It's actually an integral part of the game; thus, the United States should be obligated to include it as part of their development of the game.

This development will not only benefit the development of the game as a whole, but it will also build the longevity of the sport and the league in the United States and provide an essential backbone for the further development of MLS and American soccer as they cap out on maximum teams.

***

The other integral parts of the game that I outlined were local growth and improved soccer infrastructure. As I explained previously, the best way to grow these two aspects of American soccer would be to follow the Icelandic model. This would mean making it much easier to become a licensed coach and referee as well as providing the opportunity for more kids to play the game, which includes building more facilities and making more paraphernalia accessible, which is also a page out of the Icelandic playbook. Both of these things, however, would be local-level projects rather than the referees and coaches, which would be more nationally sanctioned projects.

All three of the big goals are actually intertwined.

The relegation-promotion process outlined would make the sport more competitive, which would stimulate local growth as well as redistribute some of the wealth from the top league down as teams cycled through higher-league soccer and came into some cash. The additional funds would make it easier for teams to improve facilities and other resources, which would not only serve as improvements to the clubs but to the individual communities themselves.

Access to more resources, whether it be facilities, coaches, or equipment, would have a trickle-up effect going the opposite way. As coaching and access to resources improved there would be higher quality players who could either be sold to MLS teams or exported to Europe or South America to raise funds. Either way, the overall quality of the league would increase and that would make the quality of Major League Soccer much higher as well, as more skilled players would compete year by year.

This cycle of improvement and progression is why America needs to focus on developing the game in a real way, rather than just bringing more millionaires and billionaires into the ownership pool to keep their current scheme running. Without changing the system, the league cannot progress further. They will be doomed to stagnate forevermore, and American soccer will never reach its full potential.

Without immediate action, without progression, without change, the athletes I have grown up idolizing, the games I have grown up watching, and the sport I love will remain "outside" and disconnected from the culture and institutions of the United States of America.

Proposed Pyramid League Structure in the United States

ACKNOWLEDGMENTS

My journey towards the publication of this book was first started in the summer of 2019 when I received a mysterious Direct Message via LinkedIn from someone who has changed my life. Eric Koester, Georgetown professor, Creighton Prep graduate, and director of the Creator Institute's program for which he recommended me "slid into my dm's" hoping to convince me to write a book. Luckily enough for him and me, I decided to take a look at his suggestion and began writing that fall. Without that initial suggestion from him, and his regimented learning sessions throughout the fall and winter providing me with some of his professional insights as an already published author, I never would have made it to where I am today.

Throughout the ensuing journey, I received irreplaceable help and advice from the entire team at New Degree Press, but more specifically Michael Bailey who helped me get my initial manuscript together, Casey Mahalik, who was the first person to help me revise the completed manuscript, Brian Bies, who authored a series of virtual workshops during the publishing process, John Chancey, who's input and encouragement kept me going throughout the entire publishing process and an intense quarantine, Cynthia Tucker, who copy edited the entire book, and everyone else at New Degree Press who I didn't work with directly but had an impact on me just the same.

Thank you also to those people who were kind enough to take the time to chat with me about the sport and their work with the sport including Sheldon Grizzle and Dennis Crowley, as well as those who were not directly quoted, but influenced my writing nonetheless, specifically Shiv Jhangiani and Bruce Shoenfeld.

Finally, a heartfelt thanks to my Beta Reader Community for supporting me on this journey:

Matthew Lemar
Isaac Sommer
Morgan Todd
Mary Chapman
Laura Neesen
Louana Neesen
Richard Burbach
Russell Stephens
Scott Resnick
Mark Lichtenberg
Ted Warin
Ryan Kruse
Emily Salzman
Scott Bragg
Eric Koester
Jess Knox
Dale Eesley
Kevin Kaminski
Thomas Demers
Mattie Olsen
Richard J Layson
Luke Murnane
Andrew Butler
Peyton Schumacher
Thomas Chapman
Daniel Kleinsmith
Diane Sands
Lisa Jones
Jimmy Winter
David Hirsch
Gregory Dynek
Scott Henderson

Jeff Slobotski
Tom Worthington
Josh Rosa
Julie Cortinas
Michael Iseman
Makayla Telfer

B.J. Bezousek
Dean Dziedzic
Laura Vranes
Stephen Seline
Todd Johnson
Tim Salzbrenner

APPENDIX

CHAPTER 1:

BlackandBlue1871. "The History of Rugby Union." Accessed July 2, 2020. https://www.blackandblue1871.com/londons-oldest-rugby-clubs/.

Footballhistory.org. "The history of football (soccer)." Accessed July 2, 2020. https://www.footballhistory.org

TheFA. "The History of the FA." Accessed July 2, 2020. http://www.thefa.com/about-football-association/what-we-do/history/.

Johnson, Ben. "Association Football or Soccer." *Historic UK*. Accessed July 2, 2020. https://www.historic-uk.com/CultureUK/Association-Football-or-Soccer/.

Parlier, Spencer. "College football history: Notable firsts and milestones." *NCAA.com*. January 31, 2020. https://wwwcache.ncaa.com/news/ncaa/article/2020-01-31/college-football-history-notable-firsts-and-milestones.

Perigo, Billy. "Why Do Americans Call It Soccer Instead of Football? Blame England." *Time*. July 11, 2018. https://time.com/5335799/soccer-word-origin-england/.

Pro Football Hall of Fame. "Birth of Pro Football." Accessed July 2, 2020. https://www.profootballhof.com/football-history/birth-of-pro-football/.

TheFA. "Driving Change with the FA Sustainability Team (Fast)." Accessed July 2, 2020. http://www.thefa.com/about-football-association/what-we-do/sustainability.

TheFA. "FA Reports and Financial Statements." Accessed July 2, 2020. http://www.thefa.com/about-football-association/what-we-do/financial-statements.

TheFA. "The FA Strategic Plan 2016-2020." Accessed July 2, 2020. http://www.thefa.com/about-football-association/what-we-do/strategy.

U.S. Soccer. "Governance." Accessed July 2, 2020. https://www.ussoccer.com/governance.

CHAPTER 2:

Emanuel, Roy. "How the Re-election Process Shaped the History of the Football league." *Football Chronicles*. August 13, 2018. https://footballchronicle.co/2018/08/13/how-the-re-election-process-shaped-the-history-of-the-football-league/.

English Football League Tables. "Final Table for Season 1888-89." Accessed July 3, 2020. http://www.englishfootballleaguetables.co.uk/final/f1888-89.html.

English Football League Tables. "Final Table for Season 1891-92." Accessed July 3, 2020. http://www.englishfootballleaguetables.co.uk/final/f1891-92.html.

English Football League Tables. "Final Table for Season 1892-93." Accessed July 3, 2020. http://www.englishfootballleaguetables.co.uk/final/f1892-93.html.

English Football League Tables. "Final Table for Season 1905-06." Accessed July 3, 2020. http://www.englishfootballleaguetables.co.uk/final/f1905-06.html.

English Football League Tables. "Final Table for Season 1908-09." Accessed July 3, 2020. http://www.englishfootballleaguetables.co.uk/final/f1908-09.html.

English Football League Tables. "Final Table for Season 1919-20." Accessed July 3, 2020. http://www.englishfootballleaguetables.co.uk/final/f1919-20.html.

English Football League Tables. "Final Table for Season 1920-21." Accessed July 3, 2020. http://www.englishfootballleaguetables.co.uk/final/f1920-21.html.

English Football League Tables. "Final Table for Season 1921-22." Accessed July 3, 2020. http://www.englishfootballleaguetables.co.uk/final/f1920-21.html.

Notts County Football Club. "About us" Accessed July 3, 2020. https://www.nottscountyfc.co.uk/club/about-us/.

Sheffield F.C. "Football Pioneers." Accessed July 3, 2020. https://sheffieldfc.com/history/.

Stoke City FC. "The Story." Accessed July 3, 2020. https://www.stokecityfc.com/club/history/the-story.

The Football League. "The History of the Football League." Accessed July 3, 2020. https://web.archive.org/web/20080411034859/http://www.football-league.premiumtv.co.uk/page/History/0%2C%2C10794%2C00.html.

Ward, Jamie. "The Founding Clubs of the English Football League: Where Are They Now?" *Bleacher Report*. December 29, 2008. https://bleacherreport.com/articles/98145-the-founding-clubs-of-the-english-football-league-where-are-they-now.

CHAPTER 3:

FIFA.com. "Hosts Uruguay beat arch-rivals to first world crown." March 22, 2007. https://www.fifa.com/worldcup/news/hosts-uruguay-beat-arch-rivals-first-world-crown-502035.

Klein, Christopher. "The Forgotten Age of American Soccer: As the World Cup sparks soccer fever around the world, look back at the forgotten golden age of American soccer—the 1920s." *History*. Updated August 22, 2018. https://www.history.com/news/the-forgotten-golden-age-of-american-soccer.

CHAPTER 4:

Encyclopedia Britannica Online. s.v. "EOKA." Accessed July 6, 2020. https://www.britannica.com/topic/EOKA.

Encyclopaedia Britannica Online. s.v. "Saarland." Accessed July 6, 2020. https://www.britannica.com/place/Saarland.

Google Maps. "Directions for Driving from Bournemouth, United Kingdom to Newcastle upon Tyne, United Kingdom." Accessed July 6, 2020. https://www.google.com/maps/dir/Bournemouth,+UK/Newcastle+upon+Tyne,+UK/@52.8263245,-3.6510155,7z/data=!3m1!4b1!4m14!4m13!1m5!1m1!1s0x487398a0b1a067fd:0x3b2ee0156ba92c94!2m2!1d-1.880769!2d50.719164!1m5!1m1!1s0x487d857e0c6f64cd:0xbe252b072a7619-1!2m2!1d-1.61778!2d54.978252!3e0.

Google Maps. "Directions for Driving from Brest, France to Monaco City, Monaco." Accessed July 6, 2020. https://www.google.com/maps/dir/Brest,+France/Monaco+City,+Monaco/@45.8750272,--0.7717024,7z/data=!3m1!4b1!4m14!4m13!1m5!1m1!1s0x4816bbe1d9925b93:0xc6488358179c30ab!2m2!1d-4.486076!2d48.390394!1m5!1m1!1s0x12cdc28900cb8ed9:0x40819a5fd8f2b90!2m2!1d7.4225881!2d43.7308084!3e0.

Google Maps. "Directions for Driving from Freiburg im Breisgau, Germany to Berlin, Germany." Accessed July 6, 2020. https://www.google.com/maps/dir/Freiburg+im+Breisgau,+-Germany/Berlin,+Germany/@50.2354995,8.3334003,7z/data=!3m1!4b1!4m14!4m13!1m5!1m1!1s0x47911b26560bd665:0x-41f6bb7a5df57b0!2m2!1d7.8421043!2d47.9990077!1m5!1m1!1s0x47a84e373f035901:0x42120465b5e3b70!2m2!1d13.404954!2d52.5200066!3e0.

Google Maps. "Directions for Driving from Moscow, Russia to Lisbon, Portugal." Accessed July 6, 2020. https://www.google.com/maps/dir/Moscow,+Russia/Lisbon,+Portugal/@46.8898224,-5.2838167,5z/am=t/data=!4m14!4m13!1m5!1m1!1s0x46b54afc73d4b0c9:0x3d44d6cc5757cf4c!2m2!1d37.6172999!2d55.755826!1m5!1m1!1s0xd19331a61e4f33b:0x400ebbde49036d0!2m2!1d-9.1393366!2d38.7222524!3e0.

Google Maps. "Directions for Driving from Oslo, Norway to Istanbul, Turkey." Accessed July 6, 2020. https://www.google.com/maps/dir/Oslo,+Norway/İstanbul,+Turkey/@50.1182382,10.1953922,5z/data=!3m1!4b1!4m14!4m13!1m5!1m1!1s0x46416e61f267f039:0x7e92605fd3231e9a!2m2!1d10.7522454!2d59.9138688!1m5!1m1!1s0x14caa7040068086b:0xe1ccfe98bc01b0d0!2m2!1d28.9783589!2d41.0082376!3e0.

UEFA Champions League. "1955/56: Madrid Claim First Crown." Updated September 27, 2014. https://www.uefa.com/uefachampionsleague/news/0258-0e6a0359223b-d180c4119f8e-1000—1955-56-madrid-claim-first-crown/?iv=true.

UEFA Champions League. "1955/56 Season: Madrid win first edition." Accessed July 6, 2020. https://www.uefa.com/uefachampionsleague/history/seasons/1955/clubs/.

UEFA Champions League. "1956/57: Gento doubles up for Madrid." Updated September 27, 2014. https://www.uefa.com/uefachampionsleague/news/0258-0e6a038665f3-d076aa2cce2a-1000—1956-57-gento-doubles-up-for-madrid/?iv=true.

UEFA Champions League. "1956/57 Season: Madrid champions again at the Bernabéu." UEFA Champions League. Accessed

July 6, 2020. https://www.uefa.com/uefachampionsleague/history/seasons/1956/clubs/.

UEFA Champions League. "1957/58 Season: Madrid claim third consecutive title in Brussels." Accessed July 6, 2020. https://www.uefa.com/uefachampionsleague/history/seasons/1957/clubs/.

UEFA Champions League. "1958/59 Season: Mateo's early strike helps Madrid to fourth cup victory." Accessed July 6, 2020. https://www.uefa.com/uefachampionsleague/history/seasons/1958/clubs/.

"Munich Air Disaster: The survivors who never played again." *Sky News*. February 6, 2018. https://news.sky.com/story/munich-air-disaster-the-survivors-who-never-played-again-11238262.

UEFA Champions League. "1959/60: Dazzling Madrid crush Frankfurt." Updated September 27, 2020. https://www.uefa.com/uefachampionsleague/news/0253-0d7b1dc17e3e-c896eaba1732-1000—1959-60-dazzling-madrid-crush-frankfurt/?iv=true.

UEFA Champions League. "1959/60 Season: Madrid lift cup after ten-goal thriller." Accessed July 6, 2020. https://www.uefa.com/uefachampionsleague/history/seasons/1959/clubs/.

UEFA Champions League. "1960/61 Season: Benfica become first Portuguese Trophy Winners." Accessed July 6, 2020. https://www.uefa.com/uefachampionsleague/history/seasons/1960/clubs/.

UEFA Champions League. "1967/68 Season: United soar in extra time to overcome Benfica." Accessed July 6, 2020. https://www.uefa.com/uefachampionsleague/history/seasons/1967/clubs/.

CHAPTER 5:

English Football league Tables. "Game Attendance Summary for Season 1919-20: Average League Gate Home and Away." Accessed July 6, 2020. http://www.englishfootballleaguetables.co.uk/stats/Report/gate/a1919-20.html.

English Football League Tables. "Final Table for Season 1958/59." Accessed July 6, 2020. http://www.englishfootballleaguetables.co.uk/final/f1958-59.html.

FlashScore.com. "World Cup Women 2019: Archive." Accessed July 6, 2020. https://www.flashscore.com/football/world/world-cup-women/archive/.

FlashScore.com. "World Cup 2002: Summary." Accessed July 6, 2020. https://www.flashscore.com/football/world/world-cup-2002/.

Lewis, Michael. "How the birth and death of the NASL changed soccer in America forever." *The Guardian*. October 20, 2018. https://www.theguardian.com/football/2018/oct/20/nasl-history-soccer-america.

McDuffie, Michael. "The Strange Story of the United Soccer Association." *PunditFeed*. May 4, 2020. https://punditfeed.com/long-reads/united-soccer-association/.

NASL. "NASL 1968-84: A review of the Golden Era." Accessed July 6, 2020. http://www.nasl.com/a-review-of-the-golden-era.

SoccerStats.us. "North American Soccer League." Accessed July 6, 2020. http://soccerstats.us/c/north-american-soccer-league/.

SoccerStats.us. "North American Soccer League: 1969." Accessed July 6, 2020. http://soccerstats.us/c/north-american-soccer-league/1969/.

SoccerStats.us. "Premier League." Accessed July 6, 2020. http://soccerstats.us/c/premier-league/.

CHAPTER 6:

English Football League Tables. "English Football Final League Tables." Accessed July 6, 2020. https://www.englishfootballleaguetables.co.uk/final/indexftables.html.

Fordham, Josh. "LOADED Newcastle Takeover: Where Saudi group will rank on Premier League rich list alongside Man City and Chelsea's billionaire owners." *talkSPORT.* May 21, 2020. https://talksport.com/football/695017/newcastle-takeover-premier-league-owners-rich-list-saudi-consortium-man-city-chelsea/.

Premier League. "Tables: First Team." Accessed July 6, 2020. https://www.premierleague.com/tables?team=FIRST&co=16&se=295.

Premier League. "1992/93 Season Review." Accessed July 6, 2020. https://www.premierleague.com/history/season-reviews/1/report.

Ramsay, George. "Newcastle United takeover will 'greatly stain' Premier League, says Jamal Khashoggi's Fiancée." *CNN.* April 27, 2020. https://www.cnn.com/2020/04/27/football/newcastle-united-jamal-khashoggi-premier-league-saidi-arabia-spt-intl/index.html.

UEFA Champions League. "1992/93 Season: French first in inaugural Champions League season." Accessed July 6, 2020. https://www.uefa.com/uefachampionsleague/history/seasons/1992/.

CHAPTER 7:

Krasny, Isaac. "Unpacking the Major League Soccer Business Model." *Medium.* June 7, 2017. https://medium.com/@isaac_krasny/unpacking-the-major-league-soccer-business-model-827f4b784bcd.

McKibben, Dave. "Pro Soccer Combine Begins Today at UC Irvine." *Los Angeles Times.* January 6, 1996. https://www.latimes.com/archives/la-xpm-1996-01-06-sp-21675-story.html.

MLS. "HIGHLIGHTS: LA Galaxy vs. D.C. United | MLS Cup 1996." October 20, 1996. https://www.mlssoccer.com/history/mls-cup/1996.

MLS. "MLS team owners: Charlotte's David Tepper joins burgeoning list." December 21, 2019. https://www.mlssoccer.com/post/2019/12/17/mls-team-owners-full-club-club-rundown.

MLS. "Standings." Updated July 7, 2020. https://www.mlssoccer.com/standings/mls/1996/.

SoccerStats.us. “Major League Soccer: 1996.” Accessed July 7, 2020. http://soccerstats.us/c/major-league-soccer/1996/.

MLS. “1996 MLS College Draft.” March 4, 1996. https://www.mlssoccer.com/history/draft/1996-college.

NASL. “NASL 1968-84: A review of the Golden Era.” Accessed July 7, 2020. http://www.nasl.com/a-review-of-the-golden-era.

“Premier League Home Grown Players rule: How does it work?” *Goal*. March 9, 2018. https://www.goal.com/en-us/news/premier-league-home-grown-players-rule-how-does-it-work/1mww3y06t775v1a7c6139l53ji.

Rodriguez, Alicia. “Carlos Vela is 2019 Landon Donovan MLS Most Valuable Player.” *MLS*. November 4, 2019. https://www.mlssoccer.com/post/2019/11/04/carlos-vela-2019-landon-donovan-mls-most-valuable-player.

San Jose Earthquakes. “Then and Now: An examination of key differences in MLS from 1996 to now.” Accessed July 7, 2020. https://www.sjearthquakes.com/clash/leaguedifferences.

San Jose Earthquakes. “Then and Now: How MLS Has Changed Since 1996.” March 30, 2016. https://www.sjearthquakes.com/post/2016/03/30/then-and-now-how-mls-has-changed-1996-0.

SoccerStats.us. “Major League Soccer: 1996.” Accessed July 7, 2020. http://soccerstats.us/c/major-league-soccer/1996/.

SoccerStats.us. “Major League Soccer: 1997.” Accessed July 7, 2020. http://soccerstats.us/c/major-league-soccer/1997/.

worldfootball.net. "USA: Major League Soccer 1996: Attendance: Home matches." Accessed July 7, 2020. https://www.worldfootball.net/attendance/usa-major-league-soccer-1996/1/.

CHAPTER 8:

Baseball Almanac. "Major League Baseball Players by Birthplace During the 2019 Season." Accessed July 8, 2020. https://www.baseball-almanac.com/players/birthplace.php?y=2019.

Bell, Jack. "Red Bull Buys the MetroStars." *The New York Times.* March 9, 2006. https://www.nytimes.com/2006/03/09/sports/soccer/red-bull-buys-the-metrostars.html.

Butler, Dylan. "MLS Classics: Chicago Fire make history in 1998 MLS Cup vs. DC United." *MLS*, May 24, 2020. https://www.mlssoccer.com/post/2020/05/24/mls-classics-chicago-fire-make-history-1998-mls-cup-vs-dc-united.

Bysouth, Alex. "RB Leipzig: How did Red Bull build a Champions League side from scratch?" *BBC.* February 20, 2020. https://www.bbc.com/sport/football/51475532.

Chang, Alvin. "This is why baseball is so white." *Vox.* Updated October 24, 2017. https://www.vox.com/2016/10/27/13416798/cubs-dodgers-baseball-white-diverse.

FBref. "2001 Major League Soccer Stats." Accessed July 8, 2020. https://fbref.com/en/comps/22/56/2001-Major-League-Soccer-Stats.

FBref. "2002 Major League Soccer Stats." Accessed July 8, 2020. https://fbref.com/en/comps/22/75/2002-Major-League-Soccer-Stats.

FBref. "2004 Major League Soccer Stats." Accessed July 8, 2020. https://fbref.com/en/comps/22/133/2004-Major-League-Soccer-Stats.

FC Red Bull Salzburg. "Club History." Accessed July 8, 2020. https://www.redbullsalzburg.at/en/fc-red-bull-salzburg/club-history.html.

Gough, Christina. "Level of interest in Major League Soccer in the United States as of May 2020, by ethnicity," distributed by statista. https://www.statista.com/statistics/1097591/mls-level-of-interest-ethnicity/.

Jones, Morgan. "Dave Checketts' son posts video of parents opening assignment to serve as mission president and companion." *DeseretNews*. December 29, 2017. https://www.deseret.com/2017/12/29/20624703/dave-checketts-son-posts-video-of-parents-opening-assignment-to-serve-as-mission-president-and-compa#dave-checketts-and-his-wife-deb-react-to-reading-their-assignment-to-serve-as-mission-president-and-companion-in-a-video-published-to-his-sons-instagram-account-on-friday-dec-29-2017.

Lisi, Clemente. "Remembering the USMNT in the 2002 World Cup." *US Soccer Players*. October 14, 2013. https://ussoccerplayers.com/2013/10/remembering-the-us-in-the-2002-world-cup.html.

Lisi, Clemente. "The short history of Chivas USA." *US Soccer Players*. May 4, 2020. https://ussoccerplayers.com/2020/05/the-short-history-of-chivas-usa.html.

MLS. "MLS once again the most diverse league in North America." Accessed July 8, 2020. https://www.mlssoccer.com/post/2017/03/28/mls-once-again-most-diverse-league-north-america.

MLS. "Standings: 1998." Updated July 8, 2020. https://www.mlssoccer.com/standings/mls/1998/.

MLS. "Standings: 2005." Updated July 8, 2020. https://www.mlssoccer.com/standings/mls/2005/.

NBA. "NBA rosters feature 108 international players in 2019-20: Players active for opening-night rosters come from 38 countries and territories." October 22, 2019. https://www.nba.com/article/2019/10/22/nba-rosters-feature-108-international-players-2019-20.

Pro Football Reference. "Player Birthplaces." Accessed July 8, 2020. https://www.pro-football-reference.com/friv/birthplaces.htm.

QuantHockey. "Active NHL Players Totals by Nationality: Career Stats." Accessed July 8, 2020. https://www.quanthockey.com/nhl/nationality-totals/active-nhl-players-career-stats.html.

Rupinski, Eugene. "The Forgotten Story of the Tampa Bay Mutiny." *Brotherly Game*. February 5, 2014. https://www.brotherlygame.com/2014/2/5/5380052/the-forgotten-story-of-the-tampa-bay-mutiny.

Scibetti, Russell. "Looking at MLS Attendance Over the Years." KORE Software (blog). March 26, 2019. https://blog.koresoftware.com/blog/looking-at-mls-attendance-over-the-years.

SCOREBOARD. "World Cup Women: 1998." Accessed July 8, 2020. https://www.scoreboard.com/en/soccer/world/world-cup-women-1999/results/.

Smith, Chris. "MLS failed in Miami before. Will David Beckham's team be any different?" *The Guardian*. January 30, 2018. https://www.theguardian.com/football/2018/jan/30/david-beckham-mls-team-miami-soccer.

SoccerStats.us. "Major League Soccer: 1998." Accessed July 8, 2020. http://soccerstats.us/c/major-league-soccer/1998/.

U.S. Census Bureau. "All Topics, Los Angeles, California, United States." QuickFacts: Los Angeles city, California; United States. Accessed July 8, 2020. https://www.census.gov/quickfacts/fact/table/losangelescitycalifornia,US#.

Wahl, Grant. "Welcome to Fútbol with Grant Wahl." May 12, 2020. In *Fútbol with Grant Wahl.* Produced by Grant Wahl. podcast, MP3 audio, 1:23. https://podcasts.apple.com/us/podcast/welcome-to-fútbol-with-grant-wahl/id1513071118?i=1000474404345.

CHAPTER 9:

AFC Wimbledon. "Our history." Accessed July 8, 2020. https://www.afcwimbledon.co.uk/club/history/.

Axson, Scooby. "When did the Dodgers move to LA? Los Angeles relocation date." *Sports Illustrated*. September 12, 2017. https://www.si.com/mlb/2017/09/12/dodgers-relocation-los-angeles.

Bogage, Jacob. "Washington baseball history: A beginner's guide to the Senators. Grays, and Nationals." *The Washington Post*. October 22, 2019. https://www.washingtonpost.com/sports/2019/10/22/washington-baseball-history-beginners-guide-senators-grays-nationals/.

"Briefs and other stuff: Earthquakes of MLS moving to Houston," *Daily Press*, December 16, 2005. https://www.dailypress.com/news/dp-xpm-20051216-2005-12-16-0512160142-story.html.

Brunner, Jim and Sharon Pian Chan. "Sonics moving to Oklahoma City." *The Seattle Times*. Updated February 17, 2012.

Calcaterra, Craig. "Today in baseball history: Braves announce moves from Boston to Milwaukee – Hardball Talk." *NBC Sports*. March 13, 2020. https://mlb.nbcsports.com/2020/03/13/today-in-baseball-history-braves-announce-move-from-boston-to-milwaukee/.

Dickey, Jack. "Lessons from the St, Louis' Rams Move to Los Angeles." *Time*. January 28, 2016. https://time.com/4196690/st-louis-rams-los-angeles/.

English Football League Tables. "English Football final tables pages." Accessed July 8, 2020. http://www.englishfootballleaguetables.co.uk/final/indexftables.html.

English Football League Tables. "FA Cup Seasons." Accessed July 8, 2020. http://www.englishfootballleaguetables.co.uk/cup/index-facup.html.

English Football League Tables. "FA Cup Seasons." Accessed July 8, 2020. http://www.englishfootballleaguetables.co.uk/cup/index-league.html.

Exner, Rich. "How the story of the Cleveland Browns moving to Baltimore unfolded – November 1995." *cleveland.com*. Updated May 19, 2019. https://www.cleveland.com/browns/2015/11/how_the_story_of_the_cleveland.html.

Garrick, David. "Chargers announce move to Los Angeles." *The San Diego Union-Tribune*. January 12, 2017. https://www.sandiegouniontribune.com/sd-me-chargers-announcement-20170112-story.html.

Google Maps. "Directions for Driving from Burnley, United Kingdom to London, United Kingdom." Accessed July 8, 2020. https://www.google.com/maps/dir/Burnley,+UK/London,+United+Kingdom/@52.6409664,-2.5350375,8z/data=!3m1!4b1!4m14!4m13!1m5!1m1!1s0x487b9042f0923d57:0x4feaa828ce73e4cb!2m2!1d-2.2405035!2d53.7892877!1m5!1m1!1s0x47d8a00baf21de75:0x52963a5addd52a99!2m2!1d-0.1277583!2d51.5073509!3e0.

Google Maps. "Directions for Driving from Liverpool, United Kingdom to London, United Kingdom." Accessed July 8, 2020. https://www.google.com/maps/dir/Liverpool,+UK/London,+United+Kingdom/@52.4604326,-2.7282437,8z/data=!3m1!4b1!4m14!4m13!1m5!1m1!1s0x487adf8a647060b7:0x-

42dc046f3f176e01!2m2!1d-2.9915726!2d53.4083714!1m5!1m1!1s0x47d8a00baf21de75:0x52963a5addd52a99!2m2!1d-0.1277583!2d51.5073509!3e0.

Google Maps. "Directions for Driving from Manchester, United Kingdom to London, United Kingdom." Accessed July 8, 2020. https://www.google.com/maps/dir/Manchester,+UK/London,+United+Kingdom/@52.4861292,-2.3950167,8z/data=!3m1!4b1!4m14!4m13!1m5!1m1!1s0x487a4d4c5226f5db:0xd9be143804fe6baa!2m2!1d-2.2426305!2d53.4807593!1m5!1m1!1s0x47d8a00baf21de75:0x52963a5addd52a99!2m2!1d-0.1277583!2d51.5073509!3e0.

Google Maps. "Directions for Driving from Newcastle upon Tyne, United Kingdom to London, United Kingdom." Accessed July 8, 2020. https://www.google.com/maps/dir/Newcastle+upon+Tyne,+UK/London,+United+Kingdom/@53.2216883,-3.1392618,7z/data=!3m1!4b1!4m14!4m13!1m5!1m1!1s0x487d857e0c6f64cd:0xbe252b072a76191!2m2!1d-1.61778!2d54.978252!1m5!1m1!1s0x47d8a00baf21de75:0x52963a5addd52a99!2m2!1d-0.1277583!2d51.5073509!3e0.

Google Maps. "Directions for Driving from Omaha, Nebraska to Chicago, Illinois." Accessed July 8, 2020. https://www.google.com/maps/dir/Omaha,+NE/Chicago,+IL/@41.5467668,-94.0243165,7z/data=!3m1!4b1!4m14!4m13!1m5!1m1!1s0x87938dc8b50cfced:0x46424d4fae37b604!2m2!1d-95.9345034!2d41.2565369!1m5!1m1!1s0x880e2c3cd0f4cbed:0xafe0a6ad09c0c000!2m2!1d-87.6297982!2d41.8781136!3e0.

Google Maps. "Directions for Driving from Omaha, Nebraska to Kansas City, Missouri." Accessed July 8, 2020. https://www.google.com/maps/dir/Omaha,+NE/Kansas+City,+MO/@40

.1727269,-96.3780257,8z/data=!3m1!4b1!4m14!4m13!1m5!1m1!1s0x87938dc8b50cfced:0x46424d4fae37b604!2m2!1d-95.9345034!2d41.2565369!1m5!1m1!1s0x87c0f75eafe99997:0x558525e66aa-a51a2!2m2!1d-94.5785667!2d39.0997265!3e0.

Google Maps. "Directions for Driving from Omaha, Nebraska to Minneapolis, Minnesota." Accessed July 8, 2020. https://www.google.com/maps/dir/Omaha,+NE/Minneapolis,+MN/@43.0850273,-97.0521916,7z/data=!3m1!4b1!4m14!4m13!1m5!1m1!1s0x87938dc8b50cfced:0x46424d4fae37b604!2m2!1d-95.9345034!2d41.2565369!1m5!1m1!1s0x52b333909377bbbd:0x939fc9842f7-aee07!2m2!1d-93.2650108!2d44.977753!3e0.

Google Maps. "Directions for Driving from Omaha, Nebraska to St. Louis, Missouri." Accessed July 8, 2020. https://www.google.com/maps/dir/Omaha,+NE/St.+Louis,+MO/@39.9346645,-94.1979068,8z/data=!3m1!4b1!4m14!4m13!1m5!1m1!1s0x87938dc8b-50cfced:0x46424d4fae37b604!2m2!1d-95.9345034!2d41.2565369!1m5!1m1!1s0x87d8b4a9faed8ef9:0xbe39eaca22bbe05b!2m2!1d-90.1994042!2d38.6270025!3e0.

Gutierrez, Paul. "Raiders move to Las Vegas approved 31-1." *ESPN.* March 27, 2017. https://www.espn.com/nfl/story/_/id/19016323/raiders-move-las-vegas-approved-31-1.

Mozley, Dana. "The Giants baseball team announces move to San Francisco in 1957." *New York Daily News.* August 18, 2015. https://www.nydailynews.com/sports/baseball/giants-an-nounces-move-san-francisco-1957-article-1.2324632.

Nickel, Rod. "Atlanta Thrashers moving to Winnipeg." *Fox News*. Updated November 20, 2014. https://www.foxnews.com/sports/atlanta-thrashers-moving-to-winnipeg.

Rieper, Max. "Losing a sports team: The relocation of the Kansas City Athletics." *Royals Review*. January 20, 2016. https://www.royalsreview.com/2016/1/20/10761476/losing-a-sports-team-the-relocation-of-the-kansas-city-athletics.

Teaford, Elliott. "Hornets on Way to New Orleans." *Los Angeles Times*. May 11, 2002. https://www.latimes.com/archives/la-xpm-2002-may-11-sp-hornets11-story.html.

U.S. Census Bureau. "Annual Estimates of the Resident Population: April 1, 2010 to July 1, 2019." Metropolitan and Micropolitan Statistical Areas Population Totals and Components of Change: 2010-2019. Accessed July 8, 2020. https://www.census.gov/data/tables/time-series/demo/popest/2010s-total-metro-and-micro-statistical-areas.html#par_textimage_1139876276.

U.S. Census Bureau. "Metro Area-to-Metro Area Migration Flows." Metro Area-to-Metro Area Migration Flows: 2013-2017 American Community Survey. Accessed July 8, 2020. https://www.census.gov/data/tables/2017/demo/geographic-mobility/metro-to-metro-migration.html.

"Wimbledon become MK Dons FC." *The Guardian*. June 24, 2004. https://www.theguardian.com/football/2004/jun/21/newsstory.mkdons.

CHAPTER 10:

Blum, Ronald. "Montreal to join MLS in 2012 as 19th team." *The Seattle Times*. Updated May 7, 2010. https://www.seattletimes.com/sports/montreal-to-join-mls-in-2012-as-19th-team/.

Carroll, Ruaidhrí. "Ice Hockey: Canada's National Winter Sport." *Culture Trip*. March 27, 2017.

Davis, Noah. "Inter Miami's long wait for a home game made even longer by the coronavirus shutdown." *ESPN*. June 1, 2020. https://www.espn.com/soccer/major-league-soccer/story/4100937/inter-miamis-long-wait-for-a-home-game-made-even-longer-by-the-coronavirus-shutdown.

Greder, Andy. "Nothing 'United' about MLS expansion teams in Minnesota, Atlanta." *Pioneer Press*. March 10, 2017. https://www.twincities.com/2017/03/10/nothing-united-about-mls-expansion-teams-in-minnesota-atlanta/.

"It's official: Seattle to get MLS team in 2009." *The Seattle Times*. Updated November 13, 2007. https://www.seattletimes.com/sports/sounders/its-official-seattle-to-get-mls-team-in-2009/.

Klein, Jeff Z. "Whose side are you on?" *The New York Times*. February 27, 2015. https://www.nytimes.com/2015/03/01/nyregion/a-decision-for-soccer-fans-new-york-city-football-club-or-red-bulls.html.

Lisi, Clemente. "The short history of Chivas USA." *US Soccer Players*. May 4, 2020. https://ussoccerplayers.com/2020/05/the-short-history-of-chivas-usa.html.

"MLS approves Toronto expansion franchise." *CBC Sports*. Updated November 12, 2005. https://www.cbc.ca/sports/mls-approves-toronto-expansion-franchise-1.530033.

NHL.com. "Teams." Accessed July 12, 2020. https://www.nhl.com/info/teams.

"Orlando awarded MLS expansion franchise." *USA Today*. November 19, 2013. https://www.usatoday.com/story/sports/mls/2013/11/19/orlando-city-mls-expansion-franchise/3646413/.

Roberson, Doug. "Atlanta gets MLS franchise." *The Atlanta Journal-Constitution*. April 17, 2014. https://www.ajc.com/sports/pro-sports/atlanta-gets-mls-franchise/HvSPqVRFe47jyYxbmMAJTP/.

Rudin, David. "Toronto FC brings soccer fans from across a diverse city together." *MLS*. December 10, 2016. https://www.mlssoccer.com/post/2016/12/10/toronto-fc-brings-soccer-fans-across-diverse-city-together.

San Jose Earthquakes. "History." Accessed July 13, 2020. https://www.sjearthquakes.com/club/history.

Tannenwald, Jonathan. "Kevin Durant to become an owner of the Philadelphia Union to make an impact in Chester, not just in soccer." *The Philadelphia Inquirer*. Updated June 15, 2020. https://www.inquirer.com/soccer/kevin-durant-philadelphia-union-owner-mls-major-league-soccer-20200615.html#:~:text=Figure%20that%20the%20Union's%20value,-fee%20Sugarman%20paid%20in%202008.&text=These%20

days%2C%20the%20Union%20do,includes%20majority-%20owner%20Jay%20Sugarman.

Toronto FC. "Standings." Accessed July 13, 2020. https://www.torontofc.ca/standings/mls/2007.

Worldometer. "Canada Population (2020)." Accessed July 12, 2020. https://www.worldometers.info/world-population/canada-population/.

Worldometer. "United States Population (2020)." Accessed July 12, 2020. https://www.worldometers.info/world-population/us-population/.

Watkins, Steve. "FC Cincinnati franchise value tops $400 million Berding says (Video)." *Cincinnati Business Courier.* Updated March 15, 2019. https://www.bizjournals.com/cincinnati/news/2019/02/26/fc-cincinnati-franchise-value-tops-400-million.html.

Yoesting, Travis. "Why MLS Expansion Fees Are so Damn High but Also Kind of a Great Deal." *The 18*. December 17, 2019. https://the18.com/soccer-news/why-mls-expansion-fees-are-so-high-charlotte.

CHAPTER 11:

Arsenal.com. "Arsenal Squad: Men Information & Details." Accessed July 14, 2020. https://www.arsenal.com/men/players.

Arsenal.com. "Honours." Accessed July 14, 2020. https://www.arsenal.com/men/honours.

Miller, Tracy. "Which sports run the most? Stats from football, basketball, soccer and tennis show who burns the most shoe leather." *The New York Daily News*. April 4, 2013.

US Youth Soccer. "Who is US Youth Soccer?" Accessed July 14, 2020. https://www.usyouthsoccer.org/about/who-is-us-youth-soccer/.

Worldfootball.net. "Arsenal FC: Fixtures and Results 2013/2014." Accessed July 14, 2020. https://www.worldfootball.net/teams/arsenal-fc/2014/3/.

Worldfootball.net. "Arsenal FC: Fixtures and Results 2014/2015." Accessed July 14, 2020. https://www.worldfootball.net/teams/arsenal-fc/2015/3/.

Worldfootball.net. "Germany National Team: Fixtures & Results 2013." Accessed July 14, 2020. https://www.worldfootball.net/teams/deutschland-team/2013/3/.

Worldfootball.net. "Germany National Team: Fixtures & Results 2014." Accessed July 14, 2020. https://www.worldfootball.net/teams/deutschland-team/2014/3/.

Worldfootball.net. "Germany National Team: Fixtures & Results 2015." Accessed July 14, 2020; https://www.worldfootball.net/teams/deutschland-team/2015/3/.

Worldometer. "How many countries are there in the world? (2020) – Total & List." Accessed July 14, 2020. https://www.worldometers.info/geography/how-many-countries-are-there-in-the-world/.

CHAPTER 12:

Anderson, David and Benji Jones. "US women's team moves on to the World Cup quarterfinal. Here's why American women are so good at soccer." *Business Insider*, June 25, 2019. https://www.businessinsider.in/us-womens-team-moves-on-to-the-world-cup-quarterfinal-heres-why-american-women-are-so-good-at-soccer-/articleshow/69934312.cms.

Das, Sourav. "Top 10 Most Popular Sports in The World [Updated 2020]." *Sports Show*. June 4, 2020. https://sportsshow.net/top-10-most-popular-sports-in-the-world/.

Worldometer. "GDP by country." Accessed July 14, 2020. https://srv1.worldometers.info/gdp/gdp-by-country/.

Worldometer. "Population by Country (2020)." Accessed July 14, 2020. https://www.worldometers.info/world-population/population-by-country/.

CHAPTER 13:

Creed, Wayne. "Youths are abandoning soccer in the US." *Cape Charles Mirror*. July 22, 2018. http://www.capecharlesmirror.com/news/youths-are-abandoning-soccer-in-the-us/.

ESPN. "MLB Attendance Report 2019." Accessed July 14, 2020. http://www.espn.com/mlb/attendance/_/year/2019.

ESPN. "NBA Annual Report - 2020." Accessed July 14, 2020. http://www.espn.com/nba/attendance.

ESPN. "NFL Attendance 2019." Accessed July 14, 2020. http://www.espn.com/nfl/attendance.

ESPN. "NHL Attendance Report 2019-2020." Accessed July 14, 2020. http://www.espn.com/nhl/attendance.

EuroLeague Basketball. "Euroleague Basketball – History timeline." Accessed July 15, 2020. https://www.euroleaguebasketball.net/euroleague-basketball/news/i/54664/euroleague-basketball-history-timeline.

FIFA.com. "More than half the world watched record-breaking 2018 World Cup." December 21, 2018. https://www.fifa.com/worldcup/news/more-than-half-the-world-watched-record-breaking-2018-world-cup.

Football Web Pages. "Vanarama National League – Average Attendance – Home Matches." Accessed July 14, 2020. https://www.footballwebpages.co.uk/national-league/attendances.

Gough, Christina. *NCAA March Madness basketball tournament average TV viewership from 2013 to 2019*, distributed by statista. https://www.statista.com/statistics/251560/ncaa-basketball-march-madness-average-tv-viewership-per-game/.

Kelley, Bruce and Carl Carchia. "'Hey, data data — swing!'" *ESPN*. July 11, 2013. https://www.espn.com/espn/story/_/id/9469252/hidden-demographics-youth-sports-espn-magazine.

Komianos, Sebastian. "FIBA AND EUROPEAN BASKETBALL – STATUS RELATIONSHIP: IT'S COMPLICATED." *Court-Side Diaries*. June 10, 2016. http://www.courtsidediaries.com/

fiba-and-european-basketball-status-relationship-its-complicated/.

Soccer Stadium Digest. "2019 MLS Attendance." Accessed July 14, 2020. https://soccerstadiumdigest.com/2019-mls-attendance/.

NCAA. "NCAA Men's Basketball Attendance." Accessed July 14, 2020. http://www.ncaa.org/championships/statistics/ncaa-mens-basketball-attendance.

NCAA. "Baseball Attendance." Accessed July 14, 2020. http://www.ncaa.org/championships/statistics/baseball-attendance.

NCAA. "NCAA Football Attendance." Accessed July 14, 2020. http://www.ncaa.org/championships/statistics/ncaa-football-attendance.

NCAA. "2020 Men's Soccer Record Book." Accessed July 14, 2020. http://www.ncaa.org/championships/statistics/2020-mens-soccer-record-book.

NCAA. "2021 Men's Ice Hockey Records." Accessed July 14, 2020. http://www.ncaa.org/championships/statistics/2020-21-mens-ice-hockey-records.

Soccer Stadium Digest. "2019 MLS Attendance." Accessed July 14, 2020. https://soccerstadiumdigest.com/2019-mls-attendance/.

Turkish Airlines EuroLeague. "EuroLeague 2020-21 Teams." Accessed July 15, 2020. https://www.euroleague.net/competition/teams?seasoncode=E2020.

Worldometer. "World Population by Year." Accessed July 15, 2020. https://www.worldometers.info/world-population/world-population-by-year/.

Worldometer. "Population by Country (2020)." Accessed July 15, 2020. https://www.worldometers.info/world-population/population-by-country/.

"2019-20 Report: Amazing College Football Popularity Highlighted by Impressive Ratings and Attendance Data." *National Football Foundation*. May 28, 2020. https://footballfoundation.org/news/2020/5/27/2019_Attendance_and_Ratings.aspx.

CHAPTER 14:

Arsenal.com. "Arsenal Squad: Men Information & Details." Accessed January 1, 2020. https://www.arsenal.com/men/players.

"Christian Pulisic, 20, becomes youngest in modern era to captain U.S. men's national team in 1-0 loss to Italy." *Chicago Tribune*. November 20, 2018. https://www.chicagotribune.com/sports/soccer/ct-spt-us-italy-christian-pulisic-20181120-story.html.

Cooper, J.J. "Ask BA: How Many Players Are in Each Organization?" *Baseball America*. August 21, 2018. https://www.baseballamerica.com/stories/ask-ba-how-many-players-are-in-each-organization/.

Dohrmann, George. "The Christian Pulisic Blueprint." *Bleacher Report*. June 7, 2017. https://bleacherreport.com/articles/2713937-the-christian-pulisic-blueprint.

"Future of Christian Pulisic: The Most Expensive American Soccer Player Ever." *The Sideline Observer.* January 18, 2019. https://thesidelineobserver.com/2019/01/18/future-of-christian-pulisic-the-most-expensive-american-soccer-player-ever/.

Kent, Austin. "CBA Explained: NBA Roster Size Limits." *SLAM.* August 16, 2019. https://www.slamonline.com/nba/cba-explained-nba-roster-size-limits/.

Lillibridge, Marc. "The Anatomy of a 53-Man Roster in the NFL." *Bleacher Report.* May 16, 2013. https://bleacherreport.com/articles/1640782-the-anatomy-of-a-53-man-roster-in-the-nfl.

Lineups. "MLB Rosters 2020." Accessed July 15, 2020. https://www.lineups.com/mlb/rosters.

MiLB. "Teams by MLB Affiliation." Accessed July 15, 2020. https://www.milb.com/about/affiliations.

"U.S. Soccer star Christian Pulisic speaks out on failure to qualify for World Cup." *USA Today.* November 13, 2017. https://www.usatoday.com/story/sports/soccer/2017/11/13/us-soccer-star-christian-pulisic-speaks-out-failure-qualify-world-cup/857854001/.

VICE Sports. "Das American: Christian Pulisic's Spectacular Rise." November 9, 2016. Video, 15:03. https://www.youtube.com/watch?v=bbiYoSk1Gog.

CHAPTER 15:

Biography.com Editors. "Pelé Biography." *A&E Television Networks.* Updated July 16, 2019. https://www.biography.com/athlete/pele.

Carpenter, Les. "'It's only working for the white kids': American soccer's diversity problem." *The Guardian.* June 1, 2016. https://www.theguardian.com/football/blog/2016/jun/01/us-soccer-diversity-problem-world-football.

Crafton, Adam. "Carlos Tevez's father freed after being held for eight hours by kidnappers in Argentina." *Daily Mail.* July 29, 2014. https://www.dailymail.co.uk/sport/football/article-2709791/Carlos-Tevezs-father-kidnapped-Argentina.html.

The City College of New York. "Commencement Address by First Lady Michelle Obama." Accessed July 16, 2020. https://www.ccny.cuny.edu/commencement/commencement-address-first-lady-michelle-obama.

GOALSIDE! "The Tragic Story of Carlos Tevez." August 25, 2019. video, 10:01. https://www.youtube.com/watch?v=ipQ76e-pASZA.

Kay, Alex. "Down Carlito's Way: Carlos Tevez on his terrifying neighbourhood, how he plans to help it, and his future." *Daily Mail.* June 9, 2011. https://www.dailymail.co.uk/sport/football/article-2001732/Carlos-Tevez-exclusive-I-turned-drugs-chose-football.html.

Lowe, Sid. "Carlos Tevez launches explosive attack on 'boot-licking moron' Gary Neville." *The Guardian.* January 21, 2010. https://

www.theguardian.com/football/2010/jan/21/carlos-tevez-gary-neville-boot-licker.

US Youth Soccer. "Who is US Youth Soccer?" Accessed July 16, 2020. https://www.usyouthsoccer.org/about/who-is-us-youth-soccer/.

Worldometer. "Iceland Population (2020)." Accessed July 16, 2020. https://www.worldometers.info/world-population/iceland-population/.

CHAPTER 16:

Borchers, Callum. "The NFL has the most protests. It is also the most American sports league." *The Washington Post.* October 13, 2017. https://www.washingtonpost.com/news/the-fix/wp/2017/10/13/the-nfl-has-the-most-protests-it-is-also-the-most-american-sports-league/.

Cooper, Jonny. "The story behind Iceland's assault on world football," *The Telegraph*, May 11, 2018. https://www.telegraph.co.uk/sport/2018/05/11/story-behind-icelands-assault-world-football/.

Gallagher, Sean. "Ballon d'Or winners and the top 10 players from 2000 to 2019: From Lionel Messi and Cristiano Ronaldo to Michael Owen and Ronaldinho." *talkSPORT.* May 29, 2020. https://talksport.com/football/295081/ballon-dor-winners-top-10-players-lionel-messi-cristiano-ronaldo-michael-owen-ronaldinho-virgil-van-dijk/.

Halakhe, Abdullahi Boru. "Is African football talent finally coming back to Africa?" *Al Jazeera.* June 27, 2018. https://www.

aljazeera.com/indepth/opinion/profile/abdullahi-boru-hal-akhe.html.

Lynskey, Joe. "Iceland: How a country with 329,000 people reached Euro 2016." *BBC Sport*. November 15, 2015. https://www.bbc.com/sport/football/30012357.

MacroTrends. "Iceland Arable Land 1961-2020." Accessed July 16, 2020. https://www.macrotrends.net/countries/ISL/iceland/arable-land.

"MLB rosters feature 251 international players." *MLB*. March 29, 2019. https://www.mlb.com/news/mlb-rosters-feature-251-international-players.

"MLS Players by Birthplace." *MLS*. March 7, 2019. https://www.mlssoccer.com/media-resources/players-by-birthplace.

"NBA rosters feature 108 international players in 2019-20." *NBA*. October 22, 2019. https://www.nba.com/article/2019/10/22/nba-rosters-feature-108-international-players-2019-20.

Premier League. "Premier League Players – Overview & Stats 2019/20 & Archive." Accessed July 16, 2020. https://www.premierleague.com/players.

Premier League. "Premier League Stats – Goals." Accessed July 16, 2020. https://www.premierleague.com/stats/top/players/goals?se=210.

QuantHockey. "Active NHL Players Totals by Nationality." Accessed July 16, 2020. https://www.quanthockey.com/nhl/nationality-totals/active-nhl-players-career-stats.html.

Transfermarkt. "Gylfi Sigurdsson – Detailed Stats." Accessed July 16, 2020. https://www.transfermarkt.co.uk/gylfi-sigurdsson/leistungsdatendetails/spieler/90466.

Worldfootball.net. "Bundesliga 2018/2019 – Top Scorer." Accessed July 16, 2020. https://www.worldfootball.net/goalgetter/bundesliga-2018-2019/.

Worldfootball.net. "Ligue 1 2018/2019 – Top Scorer." Accessed July 16, 2020. https://www.worldfootball.net/goalgetter/fra-ligue-1-2018-2019/.

Worldfootball.net. "Primera División 2018/2019 – Top Scorer." Accessed July 16, 2020. https://www.worldfootball.net/goalgetter/esp-primera-division-2018-2019/.

Worldfootball.net. "Serie A 2018/2019 – Top Scorer." Accessed July 16, 2020. https://www.worldfootball.net/goalgetter/ita-serie-a-2018-2019/.

Worldometer. "Demographics." Accessed July 16, 2020. https://www.worldometers.info/demographics/.

CHAPTER 17:

Bundesliga. "German soccer rules: 50+1 explained." Accessed July 16, 2020. https://www.bundesliga.com/en/news/Bundesliga/german-soccer-rules-50-1-fifty-plus-one-explained-466583.jsp.

FIFA.com. "The FIFA/Coca-Cola World Ranking – Ranking Table." Accessed July 16, 2020.

Pudasaini, Pramesh. "Top 10 Sports Leagues with the Highest Attendance Per Game." *The Richest*. March 21, 2014. https://www.therichest.com/sports/top-10-sports-leagues-with-the-highest-average-per-game-attendance-in-the-world/.

Uersfeld, Stephen. "Borussia Dortmund CEO: 'I don't want to see fans milked like in England.'" *ESPN*. November 16, 2016. https://www.espn.com/soccer/borussia-dortmund/story/2997552/borussia-dortmund-ceo-i-dont-want-to-see-fans-milked-like-in-england.

Worldfootball.net. "Germany National Team – Fixtures & Results 2020." Accessed July 16, 2020. https://www.worldfootball.net/teams/deutschland-team/2020/3/.

CHAPTER 18:

Brennan, Terence D. "Does U.S. Soccer's League Set-up Violate FIFA Rules?" *Medium*. February 9, 2017. https://medium.com/@terryblaw/does-u-s-soccers-league-set-up-violate-fifa-rules-ceec15f54244.

National Independent Soccer League. "Independent Cup." Accessed July 16, 2020. https://www.nisaofficial.com/indcup.

NPSL. "Teams." Accessed July 16, 2020. https://www.npsl.com/teams/.

Printed in Great Britain
by Amazon

46141277R00145